Uncommon HOPE

One Team . . . One Town . . . One Tragedy . . .
One Life-Changing Season.

JIM COLLINS

WESTBOW
PRESS®
A DIVISION OF THOMAS NELSON
& ZONDERVAN

WestBow Press books may be ordered through booksellers or by contacting:

WestBow Press
A Division of Thomas Nelson & Zondervan
1663 Liberty Drive
Bloomington, IN 47403
www.westbowpress.com
1 (866) 928-1240

ISBN: 978-1-5127-7203-6 (sc)
ISBN: 978-1-5127-7204-3 (hc)
ISBN: 978-1-5127-7202-9 (e)

Library of Congress Control Number: 2017900820

Print information available on the last page.

WestBow Press rev. date: 06/01/2018

Kelly.

I wish nobody would have to experience the loss of a child, but if they do I pray they have somebody with your strength and love for Jesus walking with them on the painful journey, as you have walked with me. I know Michael is very proud of his momma bear, and so am I.

Jimmy,

There is no doubt in my mind Michael saw your amazing strength and felt your loving touch as you sat next to that hospital bed. I know Michael is proud of his big brother, and so am I.

Michael,

Time most certainly does not heal all wounds. I feel you with me, but miss you daily. You are always in our hearts, and I can't wait to see you again soon. I can only imagine...

CONTENTS

Foreword...xi

Prologue...xiii

Part I: The Hope

Chapter 1   Memories...1

Chapter 2   Coaches Meeting – Core Values..................5

Chapter 3   The Perfect Season 11

Chapter 4   Coach MC 18

Chapter 5   More Love, More Jesus 25

Chapter 6   The Man in the Mirror 31

Chapter 7   The Ring-er 34

Chapter 8   Meet the Parents 37

Chapter 9   WWMCD – What Would MC Do...........42

Chapter 10 Our Last Practice...47

Part II: The Crash

Chapter 11 The Last Dance...55

Chapter 12 The Doorbell 58

Chapter 13 Your Son Has Been in an Accident 59

Chapter 14 It Can't Be That Bad 61

Chapter 15 Five Days 63

Chapter 16 Saying Goodbye..70

Chapter 17 The Visitation 74

Chapter 18 The Funeral 78

Chapter 19 Community = One Team 89

Chapter 20 Pay It Forward - #MCstrong............................96

Chapter 21 There is No Playbook.....................................106

Part III: A New Perspective

Chapter 22 Visit with Michael 123

Chapter 23 My Return to the Dugout...............................127

Chapter 24 MC – Still Coaching 131

Chapter 25 Game Day – Angel in the Dugout 136

Chapter 26 Different Issues, Different Answers 144

Chapter 27 He Reminds Me of a Young Michael Collins ... 152

Chapter 28 Field of Dreams 160

Chapter 29 Senior Night 164

Part IV: Spirit Rising

Chapter 30 We Believe 175

Chapter 31 Dugout Visitor...178

Chapter 32 It's Just Game Number 35 181

Chapter 33 You Were Meant To Do This 189

Chapter 34 A Life Changed 203

Chapter 35 House Money 208

Chapter 36 One Team...213

Chapter 37 Sweet 16 218

Chapter 38 It's Hard - Compared to What? 229

Chapter 39 The Last Huddle...237

Chapter 40 A Message from Michael.............................240
Chapter 41 A Saturday Morning with Michael...........................245

Epilogue..251
Acknowledgements...255

FOREWORD

· ● ● ● ● ● ● ·

The journey with Jesus that we call faith is not always what we think it will be, but it is a faith journey nonetheless. And journeys by nature are filled with victories and setbacks, ups and downs, triumphs and tragedies, and the many people we meet along the way. In fact, it is the people we meet along the way that become the most important part of the journey. This journey of life is about the destination, and the route we travel to get there, but mostly it's about the traveling companions who walk with us.

Jim and Kelly Collins began as unlikely traveling companions for me because Jim coached the little league basketball team that always seemed to beat my son's team. Of course, by junior high and high school, our sons were playing on the same team and we spent a lot of time sitting on wooden bleachers watching their exploits on the court. It wasn't long before the Collins family was attending our church and would sit week after week in our services. I always noticed them because Michael sat with them and paid attention during the sermon! He actually tweeted stuff from my sermon, which is pretty rare for a young high school and college kid.

Actually, several of us parents from this unique set of friends who played ball together became friends and kept in touch with each other as our kids went to college and moved on with life. In fact, much of this book will tell of Michael's story of baseball and faith at Heartland

Community College that we all lived together. We were thrilled to hear about the success of Michael's baseball team…and we were devastated to hear of the crash that would eventually take his life.

This is most definitely the devastating "down" of the journey, and I must admit that even as a pastor, it's hard to come up with the words to express the sorrow, hope, and love that you feel for a family. But we were together through it all and beyond. After the funeral, I remember meeting with Kelly and Jim on different occasions trying to help them piece together the death of their son with their faith in God.

It's not easy, but what I told Kelly still rings true all these years later: Our "good" is not God's "good". He sees "good" from an eternal perspective and we look at "good" from our worldly view. As unlikely as it may seem, Romans 8:28 that says, "we know that for those who love God all things work together for good…" is true even in Michael's death. As Jim was trying wrap his soul around everything involved with Michael, I encouraged him to write. In fact, I believe "Uncommon Hope" is one of the good eternal things God is doing that will live past the tragedy of the story.

This is the story of Michael's short but amazing life. It's a book about sports. It's a book about Jesus and faith. It's a story about the journey and the people you meet along the way. I'm so glad that I am one of those traveling companions and I believe that by reading "Uncommon Hope", you can be too. I pray it helps you on your way as it has helped me on mine.

Mike Baker
Senior Pastor
Eastview Christian Church

PROLOGUE

It was early spring, 2009. My son Michael was a junior at Normal West High School and the starting second baseman on the varsity baseball team. I was an assistant coach.

The lure of drugs, alcohol, and a multitude of other potentially bad choices was a constant pressure on these teenagers and our team.

I volunteered to lead a book study on former Indianapolis Colts head coach Tony Dungy's bestseller, "Dare to be Uncommon – Finding Your Path to Significance."

We met on Sunday evenings during the baseball season. The sessions were open to all players on our varsity team.

Attendance at the sessions was optional, except for Michael. I told him it wouldn't look very good if he didn't participate in these sessions offered by his own Dad.

As we reached the conclusion of our study, we talked about "legacy" and how each of us would want to be remembered.

In our final meeting, I asked the players to write their own obituary.

They struggled with the assignment.

All the papers submitted, except for one, offered a simple list of bullet point items.

Some of the descriptions were serious; loving and caring, loving son and brother, someone to lean on.

Other characteristics noted were more humorous; dressed with style, played with swag, had gorgeous eyes.

Only one of the papers submitted was written in something even close to the style of obituary you might actually read in a newspaper.

It was Michael's.

Michael Collins, age 18, Bloomington-Normal —

Michael was a good kid who enjoyed spending time with friends and family.

His favorite sports included baseball, basketball and golf. His hobbies included fishing and other activities.

He was a strong believer in Jesus Christ and helped others look to follow God. He enjoyed making people laugh until he died.

PART I

The Hope

"But those who trust in the Lord
will find new strength.
They will soar high on wings like Eagles.
They will run and not grow weary.
They will walk and not faint."
Isaiah 40:31

CHAPTER 1

• • • • • • •

Memories

"That was a crazy week," Michael said, a smile beaming brightly across his young face.

Michael and I stared at the basement wall, a wall that had been turned into a shrine. The pictures, plaques, and framed newspaper articles commemorated the 2012 baseball State Championship won by the University High Pioneers. I was the head coach.

It was now 2014, and father and son were waiting for the rest of the coaching staff to arrive at our house for a pre-season meeting. Michael was starting his second year as an assistant baseball coach on my staff at U-High. But in this moment, our eyes were on the "shrine" and our minds raced back to that wonderful week in 2012.

The framed front page of The Daily Pantagraph newspaper grabbed our focus first. The headline said it all: PIONEERS WIN STATE CHAMPIONSHIP. A framed photograph of the team in a pregame prayer was strategically placed next to a framed photograph of the players piling on each other after the win.

Michael didn't get to see his Dad's greatest coaching moment. And I wasn't there for Michael's greatest, and final, moments of his baseball playing career. Our eyes quickly shifted to the right side of the wall. The framed column from that same Sunday paper captured the glorious week.

* * * *

Baseball Puts Collins Family on Emotional Ride
Column by Randy Kindred:

Two years ago when Jim Collins was considering an opportunity to become head baseball coach at University High School, he tried to think of every scenario.

This one never entered his mind.

You don't envision the pinnacle of your son's baseball career coinciding with yours...a 10 hour drive and nearly 700 miles apart.

For the past week, while Collins was coaching U-High's run to Saturday night's Class 2A state championship game, his youngest son, Michael, was playing second base for Heartland Community College in the NJCAA Division II World Series at Enid, Oklahoma.

A self-proclaimed "baseball family," every Collins will tell you it was a blessing, a good problem to have.

Still...

"It has been very difficult," Jim Collins said. "We've all been kind of torn. I was torn not going where I thought I should be. Michael was torn because he thought he should be here watching. My wife was torn."

You bet.

Kelly Collins stayed with U-High's run through last Saturday's sectional title-game win over Olympia – while Michael and Heartland played their first game in Oklahoma – and Monday's super-sectional victory over Quincy Notre Dame.

A loss along the way would have sent the Collinses driving toward Enid. Instead, U-High kept churning toward Peoria and this weekend's state finals.

"When we won on Monday I told her, 'if you're waiting for me to get beat, I think we're out of time,'" Jim Collins said.

Thus, Mom did what moms do. She began to fret over how to get to Oklahoma, not wanting to drive 10 hours alone. Some family friends came through.

Leaving Bloomington-Normal early Thursday morning, they drove her halfway to Enid. From the other direction came Jon Albee, the Collinses nephew who was in Oklahoma for the tournament.

"He met us in a Walmart parking lot in a town called Saint Robert, Missouri," Kelly Collins said. "We met at 11 a.m."

You can't make this stuff up.

Nephew and aunt arrived in Enid late afternoon. Heartland already was at David Allen Memorial Ballpark getting ready for that night's game.

A victory would keep the Hawks alive in the double-elimination tournament. A loss would end the season and, in turn, the career of Michael Collins, who plans to attend Illinois State next year and not play baseball.

He was unaware his mother had made the trip as he and the Hawks jogged in from center field during the pre-game.

"She was in the front row," Michael said Saturday. "I almost lost it."

His impulse was to jump in the stands and give her a hug. He did the next best thing.

"He looked up and did a double take," Kelly Collins said. "The look on his face was priceless. He broke into a huge smile and waved and blew me a kiss.

"It was a sweet moment, and then he had three beautiful base hits and played a great game."

Again, you can't make this up.

Michael Collins was 3-3 in the 8-4 win over Western Oklahoma State.

"It was a huge blessing for me," he said. "Not knowing what game might be my last, it was very special to see her there. I wish my Dad would have been able to be there too, but what he's doing is a lot more important."

Heartland's run ended Friday night with an 11-3 loss to LSU-Eunice. The Hawks placed third in the nation, and on Saturday, Michael was riding the bus home with his teammates.

Mom was back in the Twin Cities. She and Albee left Enid shortly after Friday night's game and drove straight through, arriving in Bloomington-Normal at about 9 a.m. Saturday.

Kelly Collins took a shower and a nap and headed to Peoria for the title game against Rock Island Alleman, ensuring her husband a larger rooting section than in Friday's 8-3 semifinal win over Trenton-Wesclin.

His niece, Katie Rutledge, was married Friday night in Bloomington-Normal. Nearly all of his relatives were at the wedding, including his oldest son, Jimmy, while his wife and Michael were in Oklahoma.

"I had my mother-in-law and a niece on my wife's side here (at Peoria)," Jim Collins said. "Everybody else was off doing something more important."

The focus turned to U-High and baseball on Saturday for the Collins clan, capping a whirlwind stretch.

"For a baseball family, even though it's been hard being so far apart, it's been as exciting a week as you can get," Jim Collins said.

"We have nothing else all summer, but we had all of this in the same week," Kelly Collins said. "It's been a crazy ride."

Indeed.

Who would have thought it?

* * * *

"Hey Dad," Michael said, breaking the silence. "Do you remember when you asked me if I wanted one of your state championship rings?"

"Yes," I answered. "You told me only players and coaches should have a ring."

"I know," he responded. "But I think I've changed my mind. When I think about all the phone calls we had and all the advice I gave you, it was like I WAS a coach. I think I deserve a ring."

"Michael, if you want a ring I will get you a ring," I said. "I will check and see if Jimmy wants one too. I wouldn't have been coaching that team if it weren't for the two of you."

It was the greatest season of my life.

I wish I could say it was still my most memorable.

CHAPTER 2

• • • • • • •

Coaches Meeting — Core Values

The rest of the coaching staff had now arrived and joined Michael and me in our basement. Every year, I tried to get the entire staff together for a meeting or two prior to the season to review our handbook and discuss coaching philosophies to make sure we were all headed in the same direction.

This year, the meeting took on added significance because Steve Paxson and John Haws were new to the varsity staff.

I started the meeting by asking them to turn to the first page of our baseball handbook, which provided the mission statement I had developed:

> *Impact the lives of young men by using baseball as a classroom to teach life lessons and leadership skills to provide a foundation for future success.*

"Please notice our mission statement doesn't say anything about winning,"

I said. The new coaches gave me a puzzled look. "Don't get me wrong, I want to win and we will work as hard as any team to win, but winning is going to be a by-product of doing things the right way. I want this program to be about something bigger than baseball and wins."

I went to the white dry erase board and wrote one word: UNCOMMON

"When Michael was a junior at Normal West High School and I was an assistant coach, I led an optional book study on Sunday evenings for players in the program," I explained. "We studied the book, "Dare to be Uncommon," by Tony Dungy, head coach of the Indianapolis Colts." I handed each coach a copy of the book.

"This book changed my life and it made an impact on the kids involved in our sessions. I want guys in this program to dare to be uncommon. What do you guys think that would look like?"

The blank looks and nervous silence made me wonder if this would be a very long and difficult meeting, or a short meeting, depending on how you looked at it. Michael jumped in to break the silence. "No cussing," he blurted, with a sly grin and raised voice that only comes with confidence in an answer. He knew foul language was a pet peeve of mine, and common in our culture. I added it to the board.

I think Michael's willingness to be the first to respond may have touched a competitive nerve in the other coaches. I'm not sure they liked the youngest and least experienced coach providing dialogue before they did. Discussion ensued, and before long we had started to compile a pretty good list of what our core value of "Uncommon" would look like.

Uncommon
- ALWAYS show respect for teachers, coaches, administrators, players, opponents, and parents

- Our culture may find it acceptable to violate an athletic code – we DO NOT find it acceptable
- We will NOT use foul language
- We HONOR service providers – bus drivers, wait staff, hotel staff – with our respect, kindness and gratitude
- Every dugout we go into is clean when we leave – it should ALWAYS look better than we found it

We would add to the list later, but the discussion was starting to roll and it was time to move on to the next core value. I went to the white board and wrote: ONE TEAM

"I've coached at all levels and spent a lot of years in a corporate environment," I started. "I truly believe teaching these young men teamwork and what it means to be a good team member is one of the most important lessons we can teach – and baseball provides a great forum to teach it."

"You guys have all been part of great teams. What does it look like to be 'One Team'?"

Everyone was more engaged by this point but Michael beat them to the punch again. "When somebody scores a run everyone on the team greets him in the dugout," he proclaimed. It was a commitment the teams at Heartland Community College had ingrained in him when he played college baseball.

The other coaches quickly jumped in with some other thoughts, and again a good list started to emerge.

One Team

- Everyone is on time for practice and we start practice TOGETHER as a TEAM

- When a teammate scores a run – ALL players greet him with ENTHUSIASM
- When our defense records the third out of an inning we SPRINT off the field and EVERYONE not playing defense comes out of the dugout to greet the players coming off the field
- For road games we go from the bus to the field as a TEAM, and from the field back to the bus as a TEAM
- Players not in the lineup for any given game reflect a positive ONE TEAM attitude by supporting and ENCOURAGING their teammates

I was sure this list would also grow once I finalized our team handbook and shared it with players and parents, but we pressed on.

I went to the board and wrote the next core value for discussion: PURSUE EXCELLENCE.

"Our job is to help develop each player into the best player and the best person he can be, on and off the field. We need to teach them how to strive for excellence in baseball and all aspects of their lives. So what does that look like for this team?"

Coach Paxson had played college baseball and been the head coach at a small school about fifty miles west of Bloomington-Normal. He was a lifelong educator and currently a physical education teacher and athletic director at Metcalf Junior High School. You could tell he was really starting to warm to what we were trying to do here. "Being excellent begins with being fundamentally sound," he said.

"Spoken like a true coach," I responded with a chuckle. I wrote it on the board, and other thoughts from the coaches quickly followed.

Pursue Excellence
- We work hard to become FUNDAMENTALLY SOUND – understand situations – inning, score and outs

- We strive to get better EVERY DAY – on and off the field
- Players come in early and stay late – always looking for ways to get better
- We provide opportunities for our athletes to get better year round – and our athletes take advantage of those opportunities
- We measure IMPROVEMENT in players and the team – not just wins and losses.

The coaches had really begun to loosen up as we batted around thoughts and ideas. If I wanted our eighteen players to be a team, our coaching staff needed to be one, and this session was turning into a good step forward.

"OK, last one," I stated. "And this might be the toughest of all. Any great team I've seen, or ever been a part of, has possessed extraordinary mental toughness." I wrote it on the board: MENTAL TOUGHNESS.

"Every player and every team faces adversity at some point. Success is determined by how that adversity is handled. If we know what mental toughness looks like, maybe we can help our players develop it."

Coach Haws just about came out of his seat to chime in first. "Good body language," he exclaimed. I added it to the board and soon a list was formed.

Mental Toughness

- Our players demonstrate good body language in ALL situations
- No throwing or slamming of equipment when things don't go well – no foul language
- Players NEVER criticize umpires – either verbally or with body language
- We are always focused on what we can control – the NEXT PITCH/NEXT PLAY

- Nobody can tell by our body language if we're winning or losing – we COMPETE on every pitch like it's a 0-0 game

For the next two hours, we covered all kinds of ground together. We talked about practice planning, the importance of common hitting and pitching philosophies at each level in the program, and how each team would warm up and take pregame infield and outfield practice. We discussed hitting mechanics, throwing mechanics, use of pitchers, effective practice plans, and standard hitting and pitching drills each team in the program should be using.

But most importantly, we had great discussion and reached common ground on the core values driving the vision of this team and this program.

ONE TEAM…daring to be UNCOMMON…pursuing EXCELLENCE…with extraordinary MENTAL TOUGHNESS.

Something told me these core values would be even more necessary this season.

I couldn't wait to get started.

CHAPTER 3

● ● ● ● ● ●

The Perfect Season

Our basement coaches meeting broke up and the rest of the coaching staff had left, leaving just Michael and me to pick up the leftover refreshments we had provided. Well, actually, I was the one picking up while Michael watched an NCAA basketball game on TV.

As I was picking up some of the notes and papers I had scattered around the room, I asked Michael "Well, how do you think that went?"

"Good," he replied, clearly ready to focus on something else.

I decided to press a little further. "I'm not sure how much longer I will be a head coach," I shared. "Just once, I would like to have a perfect season."

That got his attention. "You won a state championship in your second year as head coach Dad," he responded. "How much more perfect can it get?"

He must have assumed that question would put an end to the conversation, because he quickly jumped off the couch and bounded up the stairs to get more to eat.

One of the reasons I wasn't sure how much longer I would remain as the head coach was the chance that Michael wouldn't be able to continue as an assistant. He would be graduating from Illinois State University in May, and depending on where his career took him, there was a good chance he would not be able to help me in the future. I had enjoyed the time we got to spend together coaching so much, I wasn't sure if I would want to continue without him.

Left alone in the basement to ponder what might be my last season coaching with Michael and my own desires for the season to be "perfect," I looked at the pictures on the walls and the memories displayed around the room. They told a story of how Michael and I got to this point.

The first picture to catch my eye was actually a photo of my wife Kelly and me with Michael's older brother, Jimmy. Jimmy had played baseball at University High School, and the photo was from his senior day.

Michael and Jimmy were four years apart in age and very different in many ways. But baseball had always been a bond.

The next picture I saw was of the two of them walking out of a cornfield, and I couldn't help but smile as I remembered our family trip to the "Field of Dreams" in Dyersville, Iowa. I pitched to both boys as they took turns hitting and running the bases on the same field that was home to the iconic movie, while Kelly videotaped it all. It was as magical as the movie.

My eyes floated next to the picture of Jimmy, Michael and me sitting together with a baseball field and a large video board in the background. All three of us were dressed in shorts and all three of us had a huge smile on our face. A picture of Chipper Jones lit up the video board in the background. The photo was from our family trip to Florida, which included time at the spring training facility of the Atlanta Braves.

If you asked either of them about their favorite part of that trip, I have no doubt their answers would be something magical that happened at Disney World with Mickey Mouse, or the Tower of Terror, or Space

Mountain. But this picture captured my highlight of the trip. My boys and I; bonded forever by baseball.

My eyes now shifted to the two large shadow boxes, side-by-side on the painted brick back wall overlooking our pool table. First Jimmy's box, with the green and gold number 22 University High baseball jersey worn during his senior year of high school and the "Most Improved Player" plaque he had been awarded that season.

Then to Michael's box. His orange and black number 19 jersey from Normal West High School, adorned with his captains pin, was proudly displayed with a plaque and program from the 2010 Illinois Coaches Association Senior All-Star game. He was so proud of being selected to be part of that game, and insisted these two items needed to go in the shadow box.

I chuckled as I looked at Jimmy's U-High jersey next to Michael's Normal West jersey.

They were rival schools from the same community. Normal West, a public school built just ten years ago as part of the rapidly expanding Unit 5 school district. U-High, a lab school aligned with Illinois State University, was not considered a private school, but operated with the open boundaries and enrollment like a private school.

I was good friends with Greg Bee, head coach at U-High, when Jimmy decided to enroll. Two years later, Coach Bee asked me to join his coaching staff, and I did. I was an assistant coach during Jimmy's junior and senior season, and stayed on for one more year as Michael finished junior high. Greg and I assumed Michael would follow his big brother and his Dad, the assistant coach, and enroll at U-High as a high school freshman.

Michael had other ideas.

Michael kept saying his friends were all going to Normal West. I thought I had the perfect argument to persuade him. I told him I wasn't the head coach and couldn't guarantee anything, but based on what I knew about our baseball program at U-High there was a good chance he could play varsity baseball as a freshman, and be the starting shortstop as a sophomore.

I will never forget that mischievous grin he gave me when he replied to my persuasive spiel, "Good luck with that coach."

We had told him the decision was his. He confidently told me he did not want to be a good player on a bad team, he wanted to be a great player on a great team. And he was certain there was a better chance of that at Normal West.

My eyes darted across the room to the "Normal West" section of the basement displays. I looked fondly at the Big 12 conference championship plaques from 2008, 2009 and 2010. I walked over and picked up the Louisville Slugger bat, signed by the entire 2010 Wildcat baseball team. We had paid $150 for it at the team fund-raising dinner before Michael's senior season.

I paused to read the framed article from the <u>Daily Pantagraph</u> describing Michael pitching a complete game against archrival Bloomington High School to clinch the conference championship; a thrilling 5-2 victory that was probably the highlight of his outstanding high school baseball career.

And the best part of it all was that I got to coach him through all of it.

An assistant coaching position at Normal West just happened to open up shortly after Michael decided to stay with his buddies and attend Normal West. Head Coach Chris Hawkins offered me the position. I asked Michael, and without hesitation, he told me he would love to have me around. I jumped at the chance and enjoyed a wonderful four years coaching Michael and the Wildcats.

My attention now turned to the "Heartland" wing of our family basement baseball museum. The photo that immediately caught my attention was a huddle of several Heartland Hawk players, all on one knee, heads bowed and arm in arm, in their pregame prayer. As he was before every game, Michael and his #19 were right in the middle of the circle. He enjoyed some great successes in his two years at Heartland, but this photo made me more proud than any of them.

I moved to some framed newspaper clippings of Michael's highlights as a Heartland Hawk. A framed article describing a game-winning hit against Lincoln College; a framed picture of the team "dog pile" after winning the 2012 Region 24 tournament, captured by his mom, with Michael in mid-flight; an article with a picture from The Enid News and Times, describing his home run in the 2012 National Collegiate Junior College Athletic Association (NJCAA) World Series, played every year in Enid, Oklahoma.

Unlike his time at Normal West, I didn't get to see much of it.

When Michael graduated from high school and committed to play at Heartland, I resigned my position as assistant baseball coach and planned on traveling around simply as a spectator watching Michael play college baseball.

Then Coach Bee decided to step down as head coach at U-High. He asked me if I would be interested in the job. Like most other assistant coaches, I often wondered about running my own program. Two of his assistant coaches called me and encouraged me to consider it.

I was definitely interested, but there were two people in my life I needed to be on board. Kelly said she was OK with it, but told me I should make sure Michael was good. It would clearly mean missing many of his college games. The conversation with him was quick, but I will never forget his response. "Don't be ridiculous Dad," he told me. "You were meant to be a head coach. You have to go for it."

I was back to the wall Kelly had dubbed "The Shrine," devoted entirely to our run to a high school state championship in 2012, my second year as head coach of the Pioneers.

The framed front page article proclaiming us as state champs; the obligatory dog pile picture of our guys celebrating after the game; a picture of Michael and me with the state championship trophy taken the day after the win during our celebration at the school; a photo of our team in a pre-game prayer; a baseball bat and helmet signed by every member of our state champion team; and the framed newspaper column describing our family dynamics as I coached in our run to the state championship while Michael played in the NJCAA World Series over 700 miles away.

I was so deep in thought and preoccupied with fighting back tears, I didn't hear Michael come back down the basement steps and saunter up next to me.

He placed his arm around me. "How much more perfect can it get than a state championship?"

"Well, Michael," I replied. "There are a lot of things about that season these pictures don't show."

"They don't show all the times I butted heads with our right fielder and all the stress it caused. Our starting center fielder was suspended for seven games for attacking an official during his last basketball game. Our starting catcher was suspended seven games for having alcohol on school grounds. Six games into the season I had a mom call me to complain that her son wasn't getting to play enough – and this was a kid who was lucky to have even made the team! I even got a nasty email from another mom after we won the sectional championship because her son wasn't in the lineup!"

"We won the state championship and that is something I will never forget," I continued. "But that season was far from perfect."

"I'll think about it," Michael said. He made his way to the couch with his drink and snacks, settling in to watch more basketball. I took the trash and leftover refreshments upstairs and took a few minutes to organize some of my notes. By the time I made my way back downstairs fifteen minutes later, Michael was sprawled out on the couch, his back to the TV and fast asleep.

For about an hour I gravitated between watching the game, watching Michael sleep so peacefully, and thinking about the "perfect" season I had asked him about.

Michael stretched as he woke up from his nap and said he had better get home and study. "We have open gym tomorrow?" he asked.

"Yes, "I responded. "I will pick you up at 6:30."

He leaned into my recliner for a quick hug. "Love you," he said.

"I love you, too," I replied.

As he got to the basement doorway leading upstairs, he paused and turned his head. "Hey Dad, I thought about your question," he claimed with a somewhat ornery smile.

"More love and more Jesus," he said.

And with that he bounded up the stairs.

CHAPTER 4

● ● ● ● ● ● ●

Coach MC

For many kids, distance from parents is a key variable when selecting a college. Most of them want to get as far away as possible. Some parents actually dictate their kids go a minimum number of miles from home for college to help foster independence and ensure they learn what it's really like to be on your own.

That wasn't Michael, and that wasn't us.

I took great pride in the fact Michael wanted to stay close to home. As our youngest son, he was the last thing between us and an empty nest. We didn't seem old enough or ready to be empty-nesters! Most importantly, he had a wonderful relationship with his Mom and Dad. That was clearly an important factor in his decision to stay close.

His girlfriend was still in high school and would be here in town. I guess that might have been a factor too.

Michael wanted to keep playing baseball at a high level, but no Division One schools were showing any interest. There was plenty of interest and several offers, but all from small schools scattered around Illinois and the Midwest. That would mean moving away from home and perhaps more importantly for Michael, conceding he wasn't a D1 player. He was a confident kid not ready to make that concession.

Heartland Community College baseball certainly met Michael's first requirement; they were good. The baseball program had started in 2005, but in 5 short years Coach Metzger had developed one of the best junior college programs in the country. Almost every player on Heartland's roster was either talented enough to play at the Division One level, or projected to be talented enough with two years of development.

Heartland was Michael's first college visit. Even though we were familiar with the campus we took a tour of the facilities with Coach Metzger, and following the tour we all met in his office.

We left the office and started down the steps to the parking lot. I asked Michael what he thought. "This is where I want to go," he responded immediately, with no hesitation.

I was worried about playing time. I was worried about him getting here and not getting to play for two years.

"Michael," I asked, "if the choice was go to a small Division III school like Augustana College and play right away, or come here and not get to play, which would you choose?"

"Heartland'" he replied, again with no hesitation.

I substituted a couple other small colleges in the same question, but it was clear that no matter which small school I might ask about or offer as an option, his answer would be the same. Before we reached the bottom step he headed back up and committed to becoming a Heartland Hawk.

He would tell us later that his two years playing baseball at Heartland were the best two years of his life. It wasn't because everything came easy.

Michael played sparingly his freshman season, spending most of his time on the bench as two sophomores who would end up in D1 baseball programs played all the innings in the middle infield.

But he did everything you would want a good teammate to do; worked hard in practice, stood at the top of the dugout and cheered on his teammates, and did the best he could with the chances he got.

The 2011 team became the first Heartland team to ever advance to the NJCAA World Series, and Michael was so proud to be part of that team.

Michael began his sophomore season as the starting second baseman, but got off to a horrendous start offensively. At some point during the first half of the season he started splitting time with a freshman, and a little past the halfway point he sat both games of a doubleheader. It was definitely a low point in his baseball career.

I was still asking about going to a small four-year school to continue playing baseball, but by this point Michael had pretty much determined this would be his last year of baseball. He would go to Illinois State and just be a student. Knowing that magnified his struggles and made them even more difficult. He pressed. We prayed.

He was the best defensive option at second base, so he continued to get chances and he continued to work hard in practice. I remember being at the Corn Crib, the stadium where Heartland played home games, for a late season conference game. It was one of a limited number of games I got to see his sophomore season. The game was tied in the bottom of the ninth inning, and his walk-off base hit to right field drove in the winning run.

It was the best smile I had seen from him all season! This one shining moment seemed to lift the cloud and give him the boost of confidence he needed.

Michael was in the starting lineup the first game of the Region 24 tournament, and he rewarded Coach Metzger's decision with the best two weeks of baseball of his life!

He hit .424 in the Region 24 tournament and could have easily been named the tournament MVP, leading the Hawks to a championship and their second straight berth in the NJCAA World Series.

Michael starred in Enid as well. He hit a home run in a game against Des Moines Community College, and then had a 3-hit game against a Western Oklahoma powerhouse. The Hawks finished in 3rd place, a best ever finish.

Coach Metzger continued to encourage Michael on the bus ride home about playing two more years of baseball. Several small schools had expressed interest and all it would take would be one call from Coach Metzger and he could continue playing.

"Coach," Michael started. "Any place you are talking about is going to be a step down from this. I'm done, and I'm good with it."

That was Michael. If he couldn't play at the highest level he wasn't going to play. And that was that.

Michael decided to end his baseball playing days and be a full-time student at Illinois State University in Normal, but baseball was still beckoning. He had two offers to coach; one from me, and one from Coach Metzger at Heartland.

Neither job would pay much, if anything. I loved the idea of Michael coaching with me, but didn't try to persuade him. In fact, I tried to convince him to seriously consider the offer to assist Coach Metzger.

Michael had decided to major in Exercise Science at ISU. He wasn't sure what he would do with the degree, but he was interested in using his degree and experiences to help young athletes. And that might include coaching.

"A couple years of college coaching experience would look awfully good on your resume," I told Michael. "You learned a lot from your coaches at Heartland as a player, and a couple more years with them coaching could be a great experience."

For Michael, the decision was easy. In fact, for him, there was really never any question. There was nothing to debate.

"I want to *coach*," Michael explained. "Coach Metzger has Coach Knox and Coach Kauten. If I help at Heartland I will just be a guy with a fungo bat hitting practice ground balls and fly balls. I don't want to be a fungo guy. I want to be a coach."

So the following spring he became my assistant coach at U-High. He never batted an eye and jumped in with both feet.

He scheduled his classes at ISU around our baseball schedule. Not just around games, but practices and off-season open gyms. In his first year as a coach, carrying a full college class load in his Exercise Science major, he never missed a game, never missed a practice, and never missed an open gym.

I remember his first official practice as a coach. I asked him to talk with the team about bunting. I was somewhat nervous about asking him. I certainly knew that he knew how to bunt; he had hit second in the order on most of the teams he played for starting at a young age, and often led those teams in sacrifice bunts.

What I didn't know, was how he might articulate the fine art of bunting to a group of high school kids as their coach.

I clearly didn't need to worry.

He was animated and confident as he shared his thoughts on bunting and demonstrated every point. He was confident in his knowledge on the subject and commanded their attention without having to demand it. His prior coaches would have been proud.

I know I was.

Michael had been blessed with many great coaches over the years, especially at Heartland, where the coaching staff had several years of college and professional experience. He must have been like a sponge those two years. The wisdom and knowledge he was passing along to our guys at U-High was truly impressive.

Over the next two years, I often beamed with pride as I watched Michael work with our guys on base running, defensive techniques, hitting mechanics, and mental approach. He was a coach in every sense of the word and I absolutely loved watching him work with our young men. They respected him for his knowledge and the level he had recently played. Because he was so much closer to their age, he connected with them in ways the other coaches couldn't.

There were a lot of responsibilities, duties, and distractions that could make being the head coach a grind. Having Michael with me at practices, at games, on bus rides, and at open gyms, made the grind much more bearable in difficult times and downright joyous during the best of times.

I couldn't help but wonder how different and difficult it would be if he got a job after finishing college and wasn't able to coach with me.

But for now, here we were at another open gym.

The Illinois High School Association governs high school baseball in Illinois, and it's calendar dictates when schools can hold official team practices. Open gyms were invented by some coach that wanted to practice year-round but wanted to feel like he was staying within the IHSA rules.

So you publicize an open gym, which is optional and open to any students, not just baseball players. Everyone knows only baseball players will show up at the open gym, but the IHSA says open gyms are acceptable as long as coaches are not providing instruction.

I didn't invent open gym, but we certainly took advantage of the concept.

We had open gyms once or twice a week from December through

the first official practice in early March. This was our final open gym before our first practice. I had told Michael 6:30. He knew I would be at his house by 6:15, and he was ready to go.

The best part about being at winter open gym once or twice a week was it usually meant going to dinner afterwards with Michael. He knew dad would pay for his dinner, and it was worth any price I paid. We would sit and talk about baseball, about college, about girls, about life.

We both loved McDonald's, but we would try and mix it up, and more often than not Subway was the meal of choice because it made him feel like he was helping his dad eat healthier.

Tonight was a Subway night.

CHAPTER 5

· · · · · · ·

More Love, More Jesus

Michael had always been burdened with a problem people my age envied – he had trouble putting on weight. So going to Subway might have meant eating a little healthier, but it didn't mean eating any less.

It was 9:00 p.m. by the time we walked in the door at Subway, so there was no one in line and only a couple of college students sitting at a table. There was no need to study the menu – we were here often and knew the options. Michael went first and ordered a foot long Chicken Teriyaki sandwich and a pizza, which I actually didn't even know was on the Subway menu. He added chips and a drink. Just when I thought he was finished, he tacked on three Macadamia nut cookies.

He must have seen the shock on my face at his order. "One of the cookies is for you," he grinned.

I ordered my standard Italian BMT sandwich with chips and a drink, and we spread out at a table in the corner.

We made some small talk about the team, preparing for the first practice, and how his classes were going. About halfway through his sandwich my question about his classes created an opening for him.

"You remember the question you asked me about having the perfect season?" he asked.

I nodded my head as I chewed my bite and he continued. "We have to write a mission statement in my Introduction to Coaching class that we would use if we were a head coach. It can't be more than one page. It's due by the end of the week."

In his four years of college Michael had taken very few classes where I actually thought I might be able to help him with assignments. He must have agreed with my limitations because in four years, I don't ever remember him asking me for help.

"That's pretty cool," I responded, enthusiastic at the notion I might actually be able to assist in this class. "I wish I would have taken some coaching classes when I was in school. I would love to see it when you are done,"

Before I could even finish the sentence he was reaching for his back pocket. He pulled out a sheet of paper, unfolded it, and slid the single sheet across the table to me.

2014 Pioneer Baseball - Mission Statement
Head Coach – Michael Collins

We will develop young men for long-term success by creating an environment focused on loving and giving, with Jesus at the center of it all.

Give

Everyone in the program should always be asking - What can I GIVE to make this team/family better?

Coaches
-   Diligent practice and game preparation

- Create an environment that allows for fun, failure, and player growth

Players
- Don't complain about playing time – work hard at all times
- Be enthusiastic in supporting your teammates at all times
- Hold your teammates accountable to do the right thing

Parents
- Invest your time in this team – regardless of playing time
- Cheer and encourage ALL our players, not just your own son
- Do NOT criticize umpires – it makes players feel like they have an excuse for failure and it is not in any way helpful

JESUS

Love

Our coaches, players, and parents = ONE TEAM, ONE FAMILY

Coaches
- Be a role model for Integrity and Compassion
- Develop and focus on relationships with ALL players

Players
- No matter what your assignment is for any game or practice – give that assignment your very best effort
- Encourage your teammates – don't demean them

Parents
- Don't criticize coaches or players - don't complain about playing time
- Focus on level of effort and life skills – not on baseball skill instruction
- Hug your son after every game!

"I love it," I said. "Why didn't you share some of this when we had our coaches meeting the other day?"

"I hadn't done the assignment yet," he quickly retorted. "And most of it is just a different way of saying the same things we already have in our handbook."

"I just expanded on my comment the other day about more love and more Jesus," he added.

"I love the fact you included Jesus in your mission statement," I said. "But have you ever heard of this little thing called separation of church and state?"

He chuckled, but kept eating.

While he was chewing, I reminded him of an incident that occurred early last spring. Just a few games into the season, one of our four seniors walked in to the gym before a practice, handed me a bag with his uniforms, and quit. He had clearly rehearsed his exit, and for the next several minutes proceeded to let me know how lousy I was both as a coach and a person.

I certainly didn't like that he felt this way and it had reached this point, but most of his ramblings were what you would expect from a jilted senior whose playing time was not meeting his, or his parents, expectations.

But one stinging barb was more worrisome. He accused me of inappropriately talking about God and forcing Christianity down players' throats.

I wasn't too worried about his vicious attacks on my ability to coach baseball; this was a kid who had come up with different excuses every week as to why he wasn't attending winter workouts, and came up with another excuse when he missed the entire first practice of the season. The final straw came when he told me he would miss the first scheduled team dinner. I told him in no uncertain terms that if he wanted to continue to be part of the team he would not miss the team gathering. So he quit.

I can deal with criticisms, but the school administration might be more alarmed about charges of pushing my Christian beliefs on others.

I went upstairs to see if our Athletic Director, Wendy Smith, was in her office. I wanted to give her some background before she heard it from the player or his parents.

She reached in to her desk and pulled out a letter that had arrived in her inbox that morning. The Principal received a copy as well. She handed me the letter. It was an anonymous letter, but was almost word for word what I had just heard from the disgruntled senior, so the anonymous mystery was quickly solved.

As expected, Wendy didn't express much concern over most of the content related to my coaching skills. It was clear she had seen enough in our previous seasons to be comfortable with my approach. In fact, she indicated the source of the criticism didn't surprise her because they'd had similar issues and complaints when his older brother was at the school.

She didn't press or pre-judge, but she did ask about the religious aspects of the complaints.

I explained our players did pray before every game, but I was not involved in the prayer and players were not required to participate. I also admitted every player in our program received a copy of the book "Dare to be Uncommon" by Tony Dungy. Dungy is clearly a devout Christian, and the book does include scripture references from the Bible, but I told her we used the book to focus on life decisions and doing the right thing. I told her when we talked with the team about the book we never discussed God or the Bible.

Having said that, I also told her I certainly didn't try to hide the fact I was a Christian.

She was satisfied with the response. She told me not to worry about the letter and said she would update the Principal on our discussion.

Despite her assurances, the letter did have an impact on me. I loved Dungy's book and everything it espoused. During my first two years we actually used it for required reading on bus trips. We would still reference it on occasion, but I have to admit I became much less inclined to consistently use the book as a guide after this accusatory letter was sent to the administration.

Michael nodded his head a few times, noting he remembered the situation, but was unfazed.

"He was an idiot," Michael said matter-of-factly.

"More love, more Jesus - that's the key," he repeated.

"Where there's a will there's a way," he added.

"Easier said than done," I countered, rising as we prepared to leave.

"I can do all things through Christ who gives me strength," he answered.

Was my son really quoting scripture to me?

I smiled as I closed the door behind us.

CHAPTER 6

• • • • • • •

The Man in the Mirror

More love, more Jesus.

Those words kept echoing in my head as I spent the next week preparing for the start of the season. Actually, they haunted more than echoed.

I know Michael wasn't being critical. But still, the words and his mission statement assignment kept floating through my mind, hanging there like a rhetorical question that wasn't really rhetorical at all.

I thought about it all week. Here it was the night before our first official practice and the words still filtered through my mind and kept me from getting the sleep I so desperately needed, knowing of the long day ahead.

My first instinct was an addition to his statement; more love, more Jesus, and more pitching! Pitching is always key and we already knew our best returning pitcher, Travis Auer, wouldn't pitch an inning all spring after having Tommy John surgery on his elbow the previous August.

But that would have been just me being glib. Michael's "more love, more Jesus" had me looking backward at my three seasons as head coach at U-High. It had me looking in the mirror and asking why none of those three seasons, including a state championship, had approached what I would consider perfect.

I thought back to my first year when I had constant conflicts with one of my assistant coaches about the changes I was making in the program, and telling him at the end of the season I did not want him back next year because it was clear I didn't have his full support.

Did I handle those conflicts with love? Could he and the team see Jesus in my actions?

I thought back to my second season and our run to the state championship. The end result and hoisting that trophy was exhilarating, but the internal drama of the season still bothered me.

Two players missed several games due to athletic code violations. Our projected right fielder and leadoff hitter was benched for several games early in the season as he and I clashed over a litany of misbehaviors and personality conflicts. I even remember reading a nasty email from a mom incensed over her son's lack of playing time - the day we became one of the final four teams in the state!

What was I doing wrong that such a talented group would have such a tumultuous season? Was I too focused on winning and not focused enough on building character and good relationships?

By year three, I was expecting players and parents to have a clear understanding of program expectations and assumed the road would get smoother, but then a few games into the season this senior quits and shares all kinds of unpleasant feedback about me with the administration.

I always said if I was a head coach I would build relationships with all my players, from the best player on the team to the last player on the bench. If that was the case, why was I only getting calls and texts from guys that had been key players, not role players or bench guys? Why wasn't I reaching out to the guy that was the 18th player on an 18-man roster to see how he is doing?

I had always told myself that if I ran a program it would be focused on developing players off the field, not just focused on wins and losses. Then how come the only former players listed on our team website are guys playing baseball in college? Why aren't we celebrating guys that are having success *after* baseball?

Was Michael on to something with "more love and more Jesus?" And what would "more love and more Jesus" look like? How could "more love and more Jesus" be implemented in our baseball program?

These were not the kind of questions I usually wrestle with the night before our first official practice, but these were the nagging thoughts and questions running through my mind.

Ordinarily I'd been pretty immune to criticism and self doubt, so as I lay awake restless about past conflicts and concerns about the upcoming season, I realized why my level of anxiety may be so high. Michael would be graduating soon, and this could very well be my last season with Michael as one of my assistant coaches.

I absolutely loved having him coaching with me. His presence made the practices more pleasant, the bus rides and road trip dinners more fun, the wins all that much more enjoyable, and the losses bearable. I treasured sharing these experiences with him.

We didn't know what the future would hold, but certainly there was a distinct possibility he would either be in a location or job that would not allow him to be my assistant coach.

If this was our last season together, I wanted it to be – well – perfect.

CHAPTER 7

· ● ● ● ● ● ·

The Ring-er

Like most high school baseball programs, we were always looking for ways to raise money. Meatheads, a local hamburger establishment, presented us with a unique opportunity.

Their plan was to select two teams. Each team would design and build its own unique burger. The two burgers would then be placed on their menu for a month. The burger generating the most sales would be declared the winner, get a larger portion of the total sales, and stay on the menu for another month allowing for additional revenue back to the team.

Our opponent in the burger battle would be our conference and Intercity rival, Central Catholic High School.

I decided this would be a good opportunity for Michael to see a different side of the responsibilities of a coach – a critical aspect but one not always included in the job description. It was also an opportunity to give him ownership of a task I otherwise would have assumed.

Besides, I didn't really want to do it.

We carefully chose a few players and assigned them to the project.

Seniors Travis Auer, Kendall Warner and Parker Schaab were all on the roster last year, as were juniors Nick Mosele and Zach Falasz. All of them would be asked to provide leadership this season.

Kendall worked at McDonalds, which Michael thought would give us a competitive advantage.

Michael told the group to be at Meatheads by 5:30 p.m.

They dreamed up various recipes, bouncing ideas off each other along with the Meatheads cook assigned to them. They received sliced up burgers and various trimmings for experimentation, trying all kinds of different combinations.

But mostly they had fun, bonding and building relationships. Michael had a way of drawing kids in, making them comfortable with his gregarious smile and fun-loving nature. He was clearly leading the group as their coach, but made it feel like a bunch of friends just hanging out.

It was certainly a fun assignment, but I also hoped this would be an opportunity for some bonds between some of our team leaders and Michael to be strengthened even further, and push us closer to our "One Team" goal.

At 8:30 I was in my car driving towards home when my cell phone rang. It was Michael.

The enthusiasm in his voice made it clear these three hours had accomplished both goals – having fun and building relationships.

"It took us three hours but our burger is built and it is awesome," he beamed. "We will win hands down, not even close."

"What's on it," I asked.

"A buffalo sauce that has a little kick to it, but is fairly mild," he started. "Provolone cheese topped with a fried egg and French fries," he added.

"French fries ON the burger?" I asked. "And an egg?"

"Yes, and it is amazing," he confidently replied.

"Now we just need to name it," he said. "We thought we better give you some of our ideas and let you decide."

I smiled as I thought of him sitting with these players for the last several hours, having fun and bonding with them. "Let me hear them," I said.

"If you build it, they will come," he started.

"We don't really like that one but we know it's from your favorite movie," he added.

"A little long," I responded. "What's next?"

"The Big Hoss," he offered, chuckling. I heard laughter in the background.

"Where is that from?" I asked.

"That's named after you," he replied. "And these guys want to know if they can call you Big Hoss."

I was a little defensive, certain the name might be a reference to my expanding waistline rather than my authority as head coach.

"No – and no," I said. "What else you got?"

"The Ringer," he responded. "That's probably what we would pick."

"Why the Ringer?" I asked.

"Because you won a state championship ring and none of the other Intercity baseball teams have one," he answered.

"I'm not sure anyone will get it," I said.

"Central Catholic will," he answered.

And the Ringer was born.

CHAPTER 8

· · · · · · · ·

Meet the Parents

We had concluded our first official week of practice. Rosters for our Varsity, Junior Varsity, and Freshmen teams had been finalized.

As I sat in my home office on Friday night, sifting through files preparing for our parent meeting the following morning, I came across copies of an email exchange I'd had with Michael at the end of his high school baseball senior season.

> Michael:
> I just wanted to let you know how proud I am of what you have accomplished this year and wish you a great "Senior Day" this afternoon.
>
> It seems like it was just yesterday when we were at the Varsity Golf banquet and I asked you why you didn't get a Big 12 Scholar-Athlete award. I'm so proud of what you have accomplished in the classroom your junior and senior years!
>
> You've had to deal with some tough stuff your senior baseball season – some ups and downs at the plate; some criticism that wasn't always fair; illness that saw you lose 10 pounds and miss prom; and of course, the death of your Grandpa. All these things have happened for a reason – and I know you will be a better person and player because

you have endured these challenges. We've already seen how some of these challenges are helping you grow in your faith – and I look forward to continuing on that journey with you.

I'm sorry if you have felt added pressure this season because of my presence as a coach. My sense is that you have. I can only hope the positive experience we've had with you as player and me as coach has outweighed the bad.

Only a few games left, starting tonight with Senior Day. Relax, have fun, and enjoy these moments!

Love,
Dad

I then came to Michael's reply.

Dad:

As your email brought tears to my eyes it made it even more clear how surreal this day is. It truly seems like just yesterday I was coming home in a freshman uniform telling you count for count, inning for inning, how the game went. It is hard to believe that I will be handing you and Mom flowers today as a Senior in my varsity uniform.

There are not many father-son, coach-player relationships that actually work but I can assure you that ours does. The only added pressure that I have ever had was that of which I've put on myself to perform. I wanted everything to go my way and nothing to go wrong. I wanted to be All-Conference and be in the All-Star game so much that I lost sight of why I truly play the game.

Though this past month has been one of the most challenging of my life, I have persevered with the help of God, you and Mom. Though I may not have showed how grateful I was over the past four years there is nothing I appreciate more than you and Mom. From the devotions we've had to the countless hours you have spent with me in batting cages I will forever be appreciative. I even actually tried to do the math of how many times Mom has washed my uniform over the past four years but I gave up.

The past four years have been some of the best of my life. As I look back and reflect two moments really stick out the most. The hug you gave me as I was in tears after losing the regional championship game, and the hug you gave me with the biggest smile as we three-peated as conference champions.

I'm sure you will forward this email to Mom so I would just like to say Thank You…and that there are no other parents in the world that I would rather be handing flowers to and celebrating Senior Day with!

With all my heart…
Michael

I love our pre-season meeting with parents and players. It is a chance to review the core values of our program, our coaching philosophies, and set expectations for players and parents at all levels of the program.

I also enjoyed them because the season hadn't started. Nobody at any level had played a single inning – which meant every player and parent was happy with playing time and coach's decisions thus far.

Every year I was the head coach at U-High we started this preseason parent and player gathering the same way. This year would be no different.

"All players in the program please stand up," I started. "Now all moms, stand up next to your sons."

"Players," I continued, "your mom has washed more baseball uniforms than she cares to think about. She has driven you all over the state so you can play baseball. She has watched games she didn't really want to watch because you were playing. She has cheered for you when nobody else was cheering. She will follow you around again this spring and keep your uniform clean. There is no doubt in my mind you don't hug her and tell her how much you love and appreciate her nearly enough! Please hug your mom, tell her thank you, and tell her you love her."

That part usually goes pretty well. Most moms are pretty good about getting hugs from their sons as they are growing up. The next part is where it always gets interesting.

"Dads," I go on, "please stand up next to your sons." You can always feel the awkwardness start to grow as they think about what's coming next. "Players, your dad has thrown more batting practice to you than his arm can handle. He has driven you all over the country to play baseball and has always made sure you had the best equipment. I don't know why it's so hard for sons to hug their dads, but there is no doubt in my mind you don't hug your dad and tell him how much you love him nearly as often as you should! Please give your dad a hug and tell him how much you love him right now."

Some get it right with a big bear hug that is always nice to see. But many end up with their hands on each other's shoulders in a half-hug with their bodies barely touching and start to sit back down as quickly as they can.

"Whoa," I say. "Those are some of the worst hugs I have ever seen! We are going to stand up here and do it until we get it right."

And then comes my favorite part, the add-on to my tradition that started last year when Michael became a coach.

"Coach MC," I bellow proudly, "please come up here. Michael is our coach but he is also my son. We hug each other and say I love you every time we see each other."

"Michael, " I say proudly, "let's show these guys what a hug between a father and son should look like."

We wrapped our arms around each other in a warm and loving embrace.

I then proceeded to share and speak to the core values we would strive for in the baseball program: Uncommon, One Team, Pursuing Excellence, Mental Toughness.

I spent the next hour describing these values and what they looked like for coaches, parents, and players.

We had introduced these core values at our pre-season parent meeting the previous year.

One parent who had raised several athletes and been involved with many different sports and teams came to me afterwards and said it was the best parent meeting he had ever attended.

But after our first five games, I received a phone call from a disgruntled parent, unhappy with her son's playing time.

I am hoping this year will be different.

CHAPTER 9

• • • • • • •

WWMCD – What Would MC Do

We were now knee deep in our second week of practice. We had begun the tedious process of communicating, practicing, reviewing, and practicing some more the various strategies we wanted in place before our first game; our bunt coverage, first and third defense options, and pick-off plays at every base. We also had to cover visual and verbal signals for all of those situations.

Of course, we also spent time on offense, defense, and pitching skill work. Each two-hour practice was packed, organized, and orchestrated to try and make the most of every minute before our opening game.

Weather in Illinois almost always dictates at least the first two weeks of practice are indoors, and this year was no exception. We had a small gym with a batting cage we used for offensive work, and a larger gym we used for defense and pitching.

Typically when practice concluded the coaching staff would gather in a corner of the large gym while the players packed. We would talk about how the practice went, what we saw good and bad, and what we needed to work on the following day.

Once the players and coaches left I would walk through each gym to make sure we didn't leave any stray baseballs, and check the equipment room to make sure the players had it neatly organized as instructed and the room was locked.

I would then head back to the corner where the coaches had gathered, and would typically find Michael waiting for me. We would walk to our cars together, and more often than not go grab some dinner before we each headed home.

But on this night Michael was not waiting for me.

I wasn't alarmed – he probably had other plans or too much homework to wait for me or go to dinner.

Then I heard voices coming from the school lounge, just outside the big gym.

I wandered to the end of the gym and peeked through the window of a door. Michael was standing with a sheet of paper in his hand. Seated around him were several players, including; Travis Auer, a senior and our best returning pitcher; Tyler May, our senior shortstop; Nick Mosele, a slick-fielding junior infielder; Kyler Ummel, our staring centerfielder and pitcher; and Zach Falasz, a junior who looked to be our starting catcher.

My controlling nature made me very curious as to why Michael was holding court with a group of team leaders, but rather than interrupt I decided to leave them alone and inquire later.

I waited for him in the gym.

A few minutes later he came through the door. We packed up and started down the hallway toward our cars.

"What was that all about," I asked.

"I was just talking to them about what they should be doing as leaders and how they should be leading the freshmen and sophomores in the program," he said.

"We used to have meetings like that at Heartland," he added. "The older guys would let the new guys know what the program was all about and what was expected of them."

"We've met a couple of different times," he continued. "We took what we know you expect of players in the program and put this together for them to share with the younger players."

He handed me a sheet of paper.

How We Do Things
(WWMCD) – What Would MC Do

All-Times
- *Have hat on straight*
- *Leave jersey tucked in*
- *No slippers or sandals*
- *Always have a pullover on over jersey*
- *High socks on with baseball pants*
- *No headphones on the field*

Practice
- *No extreme shoe colors or clothing*
- *Any pants during indoor practice. Baseball pants outside (no shorts unless told)*

Pre-Game
- *Touch a "U" or draw one prior to the game*
- *No extreme shoe colors or clothing*
- *Put spikes on at the field*
- *Walk to the field as a team*
- *No letterman jackets*

- *Don't jersey up too early*
- *Always have a prayer before the game (if someone doesn't want to join that's ok)*

During Game
- *Black socks, black belt, and black undershirt*
- *Walk back after striking out. You should be in shock.*
- *Walk up to the plate holding your bat. Enjoy your walk up song.*
- *Sprint on and off the field. Only pitcher walks.*
- *No flopping BG's (batting gloves)*
- *Everyone pick up player that just scored/bunt/sacrifice fly*
- *Pick up runners in the field. Infielders gloves together. Same with outfield*
- *Man in the hole gets passed balls and bat from hitter. On deck touches neither.*
- *Throw around = 3B – SS – 2B – 3B – Pitcher*

Elsewhere
- *Always act like gentlemen anywhere you go*
- *Put a pullover on after the game. Don't wear jersey around.*

"This is good stuff," I smiled.

"What would MC do?" I said.

"That was their idea," he answered.

"But I like it," he smirked.

He could sense I was relieved after looking at the paper.

"Did you really think I would talk to them about anything that wasn't in line with what you want for the team?" he asked.

"I just wasn't sure what you were doing," I said, now feeling guilty he sensed I might have doubted him.

"I know what you want for this team Dad," he said. "And I think I can help us get there."

I smiled and put my arm around him as we headed out the door.

For dinner of course.

CHAPTER 10

• • • • • • •

Our Last Practice

We practiced from 5:00 – 7:00 p.m. on Friday, March 28th. The clock was racing toward our season opener on Monday, a conference game against Olympia.

With our first game on Monday, we really needed to spend all of our scheduled two hours of practice preparing for the game. We needed to review our different bunt coverage, go over first and third defenses, make sure everyone knew our offensive and defensive signals, and get in some extra swings. But after sitting in on a football team meeting that morning, I decided this practice needed to be a little different.

The football coach had told me the day before that he had been hearing about some football players making bad decisions about drugs and alcohol. The football team had started off-season workouts, and he was going to have a team meeting to discuss his concerns.

Our varsity team was getting ready to begin our standard warm-up. I told them to have a seat in the center of the gym. Our Freshmen and Junior Varsity teams were already practicing in the small gym next to us. I stopped their practice and instructed the players and coaches to join us in the big gym.

"Men," I started, "I sat in on a football team meeting this morning. The football coaches are concerned about decisions players are making concerning drug and alcohol use. We have several football players in our program. I am also not naïve enough to think bad decisions are being made by football players, but not in our baseball program." I hoped I had their attention.

A speech may not have much impact, but at this moment it seemed better than doing nothing.

"Guys, look at the player to your left. Now look to the player on your right. These guys are your teammates. They are your family – your brothers. I've seen drugs and alcohol rip apart great teams.

One year, as an assistant coach at Normal West, we had a team capable of winning the state tournament. The night we won the regional, our best pitcher and leadoff hitter decide to celebrate at a party. The party got busted and they got suspended. We lost our next game.

I know it's hard. I know how much peer pressure there is and I know how hard peer pressure can be. I know our culture says it's ok. Every commercial you see during games on TV celebrates drinking.

We talk about pursuing excellence. That means on and OFF the field. It means trying to be the best you can be, and that means not breaking rules. It is against the law for any of you to drink or do drugs, so you shouldn't do it.

We talk about daring to be uncommon. Our culture may say it's ok for teenagers to drink and do drugs – but if you have courage to do the right thing, you say no.

You owe it to this team – to your teammates. We are all in this together. You need to hold each other accountable.

I know it's hard when people around you are doing it and pressuring you to join in. If the law isn't enough, baseball should give you the cover you need. You simply say I can't – I'm on the baseball team.

Is baseball – this team – important enough to you to say no? I loved baseball. I loved my teammates. I never considered doing anything that might jeopardize getting to play baseball or that would hurt my team. I hope all of you feel the same way."

I asked the other coaches if they had anything to add. They were silent – until Michael showed just how far he had come as a member of the coaching staff and more importantly, as a person of influence to these young men. Unprompted, he spoke from his heart.

"Guys, I'm not much older than you guys. I know what is out there and I know the peer pressure you face. I faced the same pressure as a baseball player at Normal West and in college at Heartland."

He had their attention. Their eyes were glued to him.

"I do have to disagree with one thing Coach Collins said," he added.

I squirmed a little bit with that announcement, but he went on.

"Coach said he knew it was hard to say no to alcohol and drugs. It's not hard. You just don't do it. If you love this team, if you love this program, if you love your teammates, if you love your coaches, if you love your parents – you just say no."

In the time remaining we had a spirited practice. We ended right on time at 7:00. Often at the end of practice I would watch from the corner as Michael hit extra ground balls to infielders. And more times than not, we would leave together and go to dinner.

But tonight Michael was already in the corner, hurriedly packing his bag to leave.

"Are we going to dinner?" I asked.

"Can't tonight," he answered. "I'm taking Hailey to a dance her sorority is having."

"Hailey, huh" I replied.

He noticed my quizzical and suggestive tone.

"We're just going as friends," he answered.

"Behave," I added. "Remember, we have practice in the morning."

"I always behave," he smirked. "Don't worry, I'll be ready for practice."

His bag packed, he reached for a hug.

"Love you," he said.

I squeezed his shoulder.

"Love you too Michael."

That evening before going to bed I read my daily devotional, spent some time reading the Bible, and then made some notes in my journal.

I had never done it before, but I felt convicted to write the name of every player in my journal.

> *Travis Auer*
> *Tyler May*
> *Brendan Bond*
> *Kendall Warner*
> *Tyler Gillam*
> *Parker Schaab*
> *McLean Conklin*
> *Bryan Russell*
> *Sam Arvik*
> *Nick Patkunas*
> *Austin Galindo*
> *Ryan Scott*
> *Nick Mosele*
> *Bryce Hendren*
> *Kyler Ummel*
> *Zach Falasz*
> *Zach Frey*
> *Jon Rink*

I prayed they would make wise decisions and good choices. I prayed they would all glorify God with their actions. I asked God to watch over them and protect them.

I had this overwhelming sense they would need God's love and protection this season.

I just didn't know from what.

PART II

The Crash

"I have told you all this so that you may have peace
in me. Here on earth you will have many trials and
sorrows. But take heart, because I have overcome the
world."
John 16:33

CHAPTER 11

● ● ● ● ● ● ●

The Last Dance

Michael was looking forward to the evening out. He would be attending the semi-formal dance with Hailey Lanier. They had been friends for several years, meeting at Normal West High School and now both attending Illinois State.

Michael indicated they were attending the dance merely as friends, not as a couple. But the text exchange he had with Kelly and me around 7:30 pm that night made it clear he was looking forward to a fun evening.

He texted us a picture of himself ready for the dance. He had on a fashionable black shirt with colorful striped tie, but clearly the picture was intended to show off the "flow" of jet black hair he had been letting grow.

The group text included Michael, Kelly and me.

> Michael: Leonardo DiCaprio or MC?
> Kelly: Ha! I thought the dance was Saturday?
> Michael: Nope tonight. My hair looks great!
> Kelly: I like it short. Sorry.
> Kelly: Behave

Michael then sent a picture of him and Jacob Birlingmair together. Jacob was one of his best friends, and a very bright pre-med student.

> Kelly: Are you with the Bone Student Scholar?
> Michael: Jacob is with the real Bone Student Scholar!
> Michael: Hailey says hi!
> Kelly: Tell Hailey hey!

His last text was a picture of him and Hailey together, ready for the dance.

Michael's excitement around the dance and post-dance plans was enhanced because the dance signaled the end of the school year. In just a few short weeks he would be walking across the Braden Auditorium stage, no doubt flashing that precocious smile, and accepting his diploma from ISU as a graduate of the Exercise Science program.

He would also be turning 23 years old next month, and was anxious to be done with school and on to the next phase of his life.

We were also just a few days away from our U-High baseball season opener, and Michael was excited to be back coaching first base and the excitement of game days.

Michael and Hailey went to the dance. After the dance, they met a group of friends at a downtown bar. Included in the group were friends and fellow ISU students, Ali Seys and Tawni Ricketts.

They all enjoyed a few drinks, so when Michael and a few others decided it was time to go, they either needed to call a cab or find a designated driver. Michael called his friend Samantha "Sam" Nelson to see if she would give them a ride home.

Michael got in the front passenger seat across from Sam. Ali and Tawni climbed in the back.

They headed north from the downtown area on Main Street.

Across town, a 37-year-old woman made a very different decision.

After several drinks at one local bar, she managed to drive her boyfriend to another bar for more partying. While there, they downed several more drinks, mixed with drugs consumed before, between, or during their bar stops.

Her blood alcohol level was more than twice the legal limit for driving. The illegal drugs in her system further compounded her impaired condition.

She was on probation for her fourth felony. She was high on drugs and alcohol. She chose to get behind the wheel of her Chevrolet Camaro and drive.

Nobody at the bar stopped her. Her boyfriend didn't stop her. He was just as impaired and climbed into the passenger seat.

They left the bar and headed west, toward the downtown area.

She hurtled the car down Empire Street at speeds exceeding 130 miles per hour.

She ran the red light at the intersection of Empire and Main.

CHAPTER 12

• • • • • • •

The Doorbell

Saturday morning. March 29th, 2014. 3:26 a.m.

Kelly and I are sound asleep. Jeezy, our Pit Bull, and Grace, our Golden Retriever, are somehow squeezed in to our bed and snuggled up next to us.

The still darkness of early morning is pierced by Jeezy and Grace barking in their most fierce tone possible, as they leap off the bed and run to the closed bedroom door.

This is not an uncommon occurrence. These two great protectors often bark at imaginary intruders during the quiet hours of the night. It has never been an invader or any kind of problem, just the howling of the wind or innocent creaking of pipes.

So I did what I always do – yelled at them to shut up and lay down! And then the doorbell rang.

CHAPTER 13

● ● ● ● ● ● ● ●

Your Son Has Been in an Accident

I sprang out of bed. My heart raced.

Kelly and I raised two boys, so we've had a few middle of the night "shocks" in our life. Once was a call from our oldest son, Jimmy, when he was 16 years old and totaled my truck, rolling it over a few times after going off the road and then over-correcting to get back on. He was transported to the hospital in an ambulance, but was miraculously released with only a minor scratch and sprained ankle.

There was the late night phone call from a state police officer when Michael was in 8th grade, letting us know he had detained Michael and some of his friends after catching them following a toilet paper prank.

Those incidents came to my mind as I frantically slipped on my shorts. All kinds of possibilities started to flash through my mind:

Jimmy and his girlfriend have been in a fight and he's looking for a place to stay...

Either Michael or Jimmy are trying to get in and don't have a key...

I was hoping it was something like these, but I had an overwhelming feeling it was something worse. I was not prepared for what came next.

I peeked through the door and saw a uniformed police officer standing on our front porch.

I opened the door.

"Are you Mr. Collins," the officer asked.

"Yes," I replied.

"Is Michael Collins your son?" she asked.

"Yes."

"We've been trying to call you. He has been involved in a car accident and is in critical condition. You need to get to BroMenn hospital as soon as possible."

CHAPTER 14

• • • • • • •

It Can't Be That Bad

Kelly and I threw on some clothes and started navigating the near empty streets toward the hospital. I tried to pay attention to any traffic, but scrambled thoughts raced through my mind.

The phone call we got the morning when Jimmy had crashed my truck flashed through my head. He had been going at least 55 miles an hour when he ran off the road and rolled over several times. He walked out of the hospital later that day with a couple scratches. This will probably be the same thing.

But the words "critical condition" used by the officer raced through my thoughts. My hands started shaking on the wheel and all of a sudden I couldn't remember how to get to BroMenn hospital.

Kelly reminded me of the best route.

When I pulled in to the Emergency area I was puzzled to see Michael's Black Toyota truck in one of the parking spaces.

Was he in his truck? His truck didn't look like it had been in an accident? My mind raced.

I dropped Kelly at the Emergency room entrance before parking the car. As I walked from the car, I thought to myself that it can't be that bad. The dance he was going to was in town. Cars wouldn't have been going more than 30 or 40 miles per hour near anywhere he would have been. I kept thinking it can't be that bad.

As I came through the emergency room doors the first person I saw was our nephew, Jon.

The tears streaming down his face told me I was wrong.

Jon is a Deputy Sheriff with McLean County. I'm not sure who made him aware of the situation, but he had beat us to the hospital. I could tell he wasn't telling me all he knew about the situation, and how bad Michael's condition was.

But I was about to find out.

Kelly came into the small waiting room. She had just been with Michael and the doctors.

Her eyes indicated she had been crying but somehow she found the strength to give me news and facts she knew I would not be able to handle.

Her strength and calm belied the gravity of the moment.

"Jim," she started, placing her hands in my hands and looking me in the eye.

"Michael has been in a terrible accident. He is unconscious. There is a lot of swelling in his brain. They need to operate on his brain and they need to do it right away."

She held several forms in her hand. "I think we need to sign these but I wanted to talk to you first."

"Should I go see him," I sobbed.

"I don't think you should see him like this," she replied.

She knows me so well. I was struggling just hearing the words.

"Do you agree we need to let them do surgery?"

I was able to nod my head yes.

And now I knew it really could be that bad.

CHAPTER 15

• • • • • • • •

Five Days

The next five days were filled with an utterly indescribable roller coaster of emotions; an onslaught of alternating crashing waves ranging from glimpses of hope to devastating despair.

Our greatest heroes often emerge in the midst of our greatest adversity.

Mine did.

Over the next five days, our son Jimmy would step up in ways we might have thought unimaginable. Each day, he would spend hours in Michael's room: holding his hand, talking to him, telling him stories, sharing childhood memories, and encouraging him.

Kelly would find strength often beyond comprehension. While her precious baby boy lie battered and clinging to life, and others around her were gripped by fear and concern, she was the light. You could see Jesus in her every day, in every moment.

These were the worst of circumstances; Jimmy and Kelly were the greatest of heroes.

Michael was hurried to surgery. Kelly and I were escorted to the large waiting room on the second floor overlooking the main hospital entrance and lobby area. We were told he would be in surgery for several hours.

As we got off the elevator, the expansive room arranged with several sitting areas to accommodate multiple families was empty.

In what seemed like a matter of minutes, hundreds of people filled the room. Family, friends of the family, and friends of Michael came in waves as word quickly spread.

We waited. We cried. We hoped. We prayed. We cried some more.

Occasionally, a hospital staff member would provide us with an update. These updates didn't provide much information beyond that surgery was still in progress, but news that surgery was still in progress was welcomed as hopeful. It meant he was still alive.

The next 120 consecutive hours in the hospital are a blur; time best forgotten. Left behind are notes Kelly jotted down in her journal, and a few images burned deep in to the recesses of my mind.

Saturday, March 29
Kelly – Journal Entry: Six hours in surgery. Vital signs are good.

My nieces, Christina and Sarah, are with me in the hospital chapel. We sit in silence. We pray in silence. The warmth of the stained glass windows with etched faces of the apostles was in stark contrast to the cold marble floor. As we left, a prayer box sat on a table near the exit. I simply wrote "Michael" on a sheet of paper and dropped it in the box.

Kelly – Journal Entry: They will keep him in a medically induced coma – trying to prevent swelling.

Fear and cowardice has gripped me from the very moment that doorbell rang. I finally summoned enough courage to go and see my baby boy. I walk deliberately down the hall, afraid of what I will see. I get through the door but collapse on the chair beside his bed. His head is heavily bandaged. There are tubes everywhere. The rhythmic hum of the machine breathing for him. I am drawn to my "Dare to be Uncommon" bracelet I had asked Kelly to place on his wrist this morning.

I tell him I love him. I tell him to be strong. I beg him not to leave us. I tell him I won't go back and coach without him.

Sunday, March 30
Kelly: Good news – vital signs are still strong. Bad news – there is increased pressure in the brain.

They have moved our family from the expansive public waiting room to a more secluded space. The early morning sun is just beginning to bring light through the tall windows that line the narrow hallway. The cold, tiled hallway is empty except for one lone person curled up on two chairs pulled together to form a makeshift bed. It is Colton Moore. He has spent the night in this fetal position, covered only by a jacket. Just a few short months ago he and Michael danced with unbridled joy at Colton's wedding.

Kelly – Journal Entry: They are working to reduce the pressure. Pray the meds work to reduce the pressure as another surgery has been mentioned, as a last resort, to remove more skull.

Chris Hawkins, Dave Rodgers, and Nate Metzger are huddled together in the waiting room, standing near the balcony overlooking the main hospital entrance and lobby. They are sharing "Michael" stories.

Coach Hawkins was Michael's head coach at Normal West. Coach Rodgers was his pitching coach at Normal West. Coach Metzger was Michael's seventh grade coach at Parkside Junior High School, and would coach him again at Heartland Community College.

This group of men had such an impact on Michael's life, helping to mold and shape him into the young man he has become.

But tonight, they stand here as helpless as the rest of us. They are used to being in control. This is out of their hands.

Monday, March 31

Kelly – Journal Entry: They moved a bolt and meds have brought his pressure down.

The entire U-High varsity baseball team is standing in front of me in the waiting room. A game ball is handed to me, signed by all of them after our season-opening win. The smiles on their innocent faces tell of a win. The glimmer in their eyes tell of hope – an expectation that Michael will soon walk out of here and we will all be back in the dugout together.

Kelly – Journal Entry: He has taken a turn for the worse. A second surgery is needed. It would be a last ditch effort to save him. Dr. Stroink asked if we wanted to proceed with a second surgery. She cannot provide any answers about his quality of life even if the surgery is successful.

I throw myself on the ground. Tears and screams of desperation and anger burst from me. In my fist, I clutch the cross somebody had given me the first day in the hospital, but then slam it on the floor. I feel hands on my back, intended to provide comfort. Thoughts spew from my mouth as I writhe on the floor in indescribable agony; what will his life be like if he survives this…he wouldn't want to live like that…what are we supposed to do?

Kelly – Journal Entry: He is out of the second surgery. They have cut off all visitors to one. I am allowed to stay on the couch at all times with no talking. So since I know this is it I'm not leaving him.

My sister Susie is a nurse. She has been a Godsend as an intermediary between the doctors and us, often de-coding the mysterious medical language into more simple terms. She has wonderfully walked the delicate balance between truthfulness and encouragement. But the look on her face has changed. I don't see as much hope in her eyes.

Kelly – Journal Entry: Pressure on his brain is high – which is bad. Dr. Stroink says he will declare himself in the next 24 hours. She says after the brain stops swelling we will see what is left.

It is 11:30 pm. The hospital is quiet. In the hallway outside our family room, a large group gathers, not wanting to leave. Perhaps they are afraid to leave. Aunts, uncles and cousins sit in makeshift groups. They use what chairs they can find, but many sprawl out on the floor. Some try to sleep. Others whisper in hushed tones.

My sisters Susie and Sharon, and my brother Jeff and his wife Jane are here. All of their kids – Michael's cousins – surround them. Kelly's brother Terry and his wife Sandy are still here, and their kids.

Two families have become one. Scarred and bonded together – forever.

Tuesday, April 1

Kelly – Journal Entry: The neurology team evaluates him before Dr. Stroink.

Jimmy learns first. It is over.
But I already knew, as there was no more fight in him.
We meet with Gift of Hope, an organ donation company, in the afternoon.

We sit across from a Gift of Hope representative in the private room not far from Michael's room. Michael had registered to be an organ donor. We are told what that means. Kelly continues to think clearly. My questions clearly indicate I am more erratic. Did he even know he was signed up? Do we have the right to say no?

Kelly calms me with a story.

Michael was in college, living with his cousins near the Heartland campus. A notice arrived at our house and Kelly noticed it indicated he had signed up to be an organ donor.

One day Michael stopped by to pick something up. He breezed by, headed upstairs to his old room.

"Did you realize you signed up to be an organ donor?" Kelly called toward his room.

"Of course I knew," came the reply.

"Don't you think we should talk about it?" she responded.

"What is there to talk about," he answered. "It's the right thing to do."

And with that, he hugged his mom, told her he loved her, and breezed back out the door.

Wednesday, April 2

Kelly – Journal Entry: We signed the Gift of Hope documents. Michael has always been a giver – and he will give even in his death.

Family and friends gather in a circle around a flagpole in front of the hospital. Jimmy wraps his arm around his mom as she addresses the gathering. Everyone joins hands to make a large enclosed circle. The circle includes many of the doctors and nurses who have spent the last four days trying to save Michael's life. Our dear friend and Eastview Christian Church Pastor, Nicki Green, prays aloud. Jimmy raises the "Gift of Hope" flag. The white flag with the "Donate Life" symbol flaps in a chilling breeze under the purple Advocate BroMenn Healthcare hospital flag. Michael loves purple.

Many tears are shed as the ceremony memorializes our dear Michael the giving donor, but also commemorates new life and new hope for the recipients.

Kelly – Journal Entry: How do you say goodbye to your son?

Kelly and Jimmy spend most of the day leading a steady stream of family and friends into Michael's room, offering them a chance to say goodbye.

Now it is our turn.

Jimmy sits on one side of the bed holding Michael's hand, talking to him through sobs. Kelly climbs into the bed next to Michael, knowing it will be the last time she can lay by his side on this earth.

I take the state championship ring off my finger and place it on his hand.

CHAPTER 16

• • • • • • •

Saying Goodbye

Webster defines surreal as "very strange or unusual; having the quality of a dream."

There are no words to describe the last five days, nor what we were about to go through.

Except it wasn't a dream.

It was a nightmare.

And we were living it.

Michael's gift of organ donation required a defined schedule and scientific regimen. A surgical team had to be assembled and scheduled. Coolers were meticulously prepared for the specific organs. Planes were on standby to transport the organs to the arranged destinations. Desperate recipients anxiously awaited their gift of new life.

The surgical team was scheduled for 9:00 p.m.

Jimmy spent most of the day in the room, holding his brother's hand. Talking to him. Asking for a miracle.

Kelly spent most of the day escorting family and close friends into the room so they could tell Michael "goodbye".

I spent most of the day curled up on a couch in the secluded family waiting room, mired and wallowing in grief and unbelief that Michael wasn't coming back.

At 8:45 p.m. we gathered our family together in a large private room. Mike Baker, our Pastor at Eastview Christian Church, led us in prayer.

Then we began the walk down the long second floor hallway. We headed toward the room where the surgical team, and Michael, was waiting.

We passed through an atrium waiting area. Long glass windows extended from the bottom floor. Hundreds of people were gathered outside, lighting the night with candles held in vigil.

The surgical team could wait a few minutes.

Kelly and I went down the stairs and into the chilly night air. Coach Metzger and his wife Sarah were near the door. Several of Michael's former Heartland baseball teammates were near them.

We hugged as many people as we could. Few words were exchanged.

About all we could get out was "thanks for being here."

Surreal indeed.

It was almost as if this detour could change something.

But it couldn't.

We made our way back up the stairs and followed the nurses to the room.

Michael was now surrounded by his family ready to help him pass into the hands of his Lord and Savior. Kelly and I; brother Jimmy and his girlfriend Abby; his devoted cousin Jon; his Grandma Betty; Pastor Mike and his wife Sara.

Jimmy held Michael's hand on one side of the bed with Abby, Jon and Grandma.

Kelly held his other hand as Mike and Sara placed one hand on Kelly and one hand on Michael.

I stood at the end of the bed touching both of his legs.

The doctors and Gift of Hope personnel had let us know there was only a certain window of time allowed between the ventilator being removed and Michael passing in order for the organs to be useful.

We had spent the last five days praying for a miracle, pleading with Michael to keep fighting, and pleading with God to bring him back to us.

We now asked Michael to not fight for breath, praying he would go peacefully.

At 9:00 p.m. the ventilator was removed.

As it was being removed Carrie Underwood's rendition of "How Great Thou Art" played in the background, and we did the best we could through our tears to sing to Michael in worship to our God.

> *O Lord my God, when I in awesome wonder*
> *Consider all the worlds Thy Hands have made;*
> *I see the stars, I hear the rolling thunder,*
> *Thy Power throughout the universe displayed*
>
> *Then sings my soul, My Savior God, to Thee,*
> *How great Thou art, how great Thou art.*
> *Then sings my soul, My Savior God, to Thee,*
> *How great Thou art, how great Thou art!*

At 9:02 p.m., after a couple last reflexive gasps, our precious Michael passed.

Kelly and I had vowed not to leave the hospital until Michael did; so we spent one more night in the hospital family room.

We got up early the next morning. We checked to make sure everything had gone as planned during the night.

After five days surrounded by family and friends, we left the hospital alone.

We walked down the long hall leading to the hospital exit lost in thought.

There were plans to be made for Michael's visitation and funeral.

We got to the door and prepared ourselves to go back out into the world.

A world now without our precious Michael.

Kelly and I held each other tightly as we left the hospital. As seemed fitting, it was a dark and dreary day.

We left the hospital knowing we would bear the burden of missing Michael every single day for the rest of our lives.

We left there knowing we would look for signs every day, something to assure us he is ok.

Just a few steps outside the hospital door we both stopped.

We heard rolling thunder.

How great thou art indeed.

CHAPTER 17

● ● ● ● ● ● ●

The Visitation

The visitation service was scheduled for Wednesday evening at Eastview Christian Church.

What do a husband and wife say to each other as they drive to a visitation service for their 22-year-old son?

The ride was mostly silent. We simply held hands.

The silence in the quiet car was broken as we turned in to the church entrance.

Kelly gasped.

The winding driveway leading from the entrance up to the church is about a quarter of a mile long. It had been lined on both sides with hundreds of yard signs.

The bold black print against a white background on each sign read "19 #MCstrong."

An anonymous donor had supplied the markers, greeting visitors with this dramatic and touching tribute along the entrances to both the front and back parking lots on each side of the church.

Kelly was prepared for what would greet us inside the church. She had planned it, and helped set everything up.

I was not prepared.

Several of our favorite photographs had been enlarged to poster size and placed on easels in the beautiful two-story atrium leading to the sanctuary. Michael in his Normal West jersey making a spectacular diving catch; Michael in a sand trap, the golf ball captured on film in mid-flight, with a perfect splash of sand; Michael in his Heartland Hawks uniform, an acrobatic mid-air leap in the middle of a great play.

All of the pictures were brought to life in stunning color with brilliant clarity and detail. If Michael could have picked the pictures, there is no doubt these would be ones he would choose.

Especially since his mom was behind the lens for all of them.

Several scrapbooks filled with photos and newspaper clippings lined a long table in front of the sanctuary. They captured the story of Michael's life, from birth to present. Michael loved looking at these scrapbooks over the years as his mom painstakingly created and delicately crafted each one.

She expected Michael, his wife, and his children would enjoy them long after we were gone.

I did not spend any time at the table.

I had flipped through these treasures often over the years. To have any chance of making it through this service, I knew I couldn't start turning those pages now.

Kelly and I were first inside the sanctuary.

More tables of memories were set up for passersby to view while waiting in the receiving line. The various baseball hats he had worn over the years; Normal West, Heartland Hawks, Lexington Snipes, Bloomington Gold, Twin City Bulls.

There were several framed family photos, including one of Michael, Jimmy and me taken this past fall – all three of us with Titleist golf hats and big smiles after a rare round of golf together.

Michael's Titleist golf bag was strategically placed right next to the casket. He had developed such a passion for the game once he had stopped playing baseball; the latest Titleist golf clubs, a gift from Grandma; his favorite Scotty Cameron putter; his driver adorned with his ever-present pony headcover and its brightly rainbow-colored mane.

And at rest on top of the golf clubs was a book; Tony Dungy's "Dare to be Uncommon" daily devotional.

He had recently told us that he kept this book in a place where he knew he would read it every day.

We found it in his bathroom.

And there was our sweet baby, his lifeless body lying in the casket; tan golf slacks fashionably paired with one of his favorite quarter-zip golf pullovers; his favorite Titleist golf stocking cap strategically hiding his injuries; his stylish white G-Shock wristwatch; my U-High state championship ring on his right hand.

I didn't get a chance to buy him his own ring as he had suggested, so I gave him mine.

We gathered the family in a room just off the sanctuary before opening the doors at 4:00 p.m. for the service to begin.

Kelly continued to draw amazing strength from her incredible faith in God. She was determined to make this a celebration of her precious Michael's life more than a depressing farewell.

Nicki Green shared an inspiring prayer. Kelly then asked all the family members gathered to huddle close and put our hands together in the middle.

"MC on three," she said, and then led us.

"One, two, three – MC!" we chanted.

It was estimated well over 2,000 people attended. Some sat patiently in the sanctuary chairs for more than two hours, waiting to speak to us before passing the casket.

Hundreds of photos commemorating Michael's life continuously streamed across expansive video screens inside the spacious sanctuary, accompanied by a string of Michael's favorite songs hand-picked from his personal playlists.

Kelly, Jimmy and I stood next to the casket, shaking hands and hugging the thousands filing past.

There are simply no words to describe standing next to a casket holding your precious 22-year-old son.

I won't even try.

There were many difficult and emotional moments during those four plus hours, but one came closer to bringing me to my knees more than any other.

My eighteen U-High varsity baseball players and coaches showed up together. One by one they came through the line. One by one they hugged Jimmy, then Kelly, then me. The hugs were long and tight. Tears filled their eyes. One by one they approached the casket.

It felt like watching eighteen of my own kids, having to say goodbye to their brother, coach, and friend.

One team.

CHAPTER 18

● ● ● ● ● ● ●

The Funeral

Kelly scripted the most amazing funeral service.

I was still in an absolute fog of despair, barely able to function. She almost single-handedly prepared the entire service. She worked with Senior Pastor Mike Baker to determine the flow of the service and relevant scriptures. She selected the songs we wanted played and worked with a church technician to make sure they were queued up correctly.

Our family entered the sanctuary as the song "Blessings" by Laura Story, one of Michael's favorite songs, softly played.

> *We pray for healing, for prosperity*
> *We pray for Your mighty hand to ease our suffering*
> *And all the while, You hear each spoken need*
> *Yet love is way too much to give us lesser things*
>
> *"Cause what if your blessings come through rain drops*
> *What if Your healing comes through tears*
> *What if a thousand sleepless nights are what it takes to know You're near*
> *What if trials of this life are Your mercies in disguise…*

Pastor Mike started the service. We have all been to services where the pastor didn't really know the deceased all that well, and the remarks can't help but take on a distant and impersonal tone reflective of a limited relationship between the preacher and departed.

This was not the case today.

Mike Baker had watched Michael grow up. His son, Caleb, played basketball with Michael in junior high and high school. Kelly and I had sat in many bleachers with Mike and his wife Sara, cheering on the boys.

Michael had recently watched as Pastor Mike baptized Kelly and me together by immersion on our 30th wedding anniversary in an expression of our faith and commitment to our church.

Mike fought back tears as he shared his memories of Michael, including one of his personal favorites – Michael's game-winning shot at the buzzer to win a Normal West freshman basketball game several years ago. He recalled celebrating that joyous moment with Kelly and me in the bleachers.

"Michael was passionate about many things," Mike said, "but the greatest joy he brought his family was his faith in God and his relationship with the Lord. His favorite scripture was Philippians 4:13, 'For I can do everything through Christ, who gives me strength.'"

Mike then preached a wonderful mini-sermon with a very simple message; we don't have all the answers, but God does. He ended with scripture from Isaiah.

"My thoughts are nothing like your thoughts," says the Lord. "And my ways are far beyond anything you could imagine. For just as the heavens are higher than the earth, so my ways are higher than your ways and my thoughts higher than your thoughts."

As Mike sat down, the timeless Christian classic "Imagine" by Mercy Me faded in through the giant speakers.

> I can only imagine what it will be like
> When I walk by your side
> I can only imagine what my eyes will see

When your face is before me
I can only imagine...

Nate Metzger was next on the stage. Michael loved being a Heartland Hawk and he loved Coach Metzger.

"We knew Michael was interested in playing at Heartland," Metzger started. "But to be honest, we weren't all that interested in him. In fact, I had told Michael we were looking at several middle infielders ahead of him and he should look at other options."

"We held a showcase event for college coaches at Heartland in the fall and Michael attended. After the event Michael sought me out, shook my hand, and told me thanks for inviting him to participate. This was just a few weeks after I told him we weren't all that interested. I decided right there he was the kind of kid I wanted in our program."

As if talking about his own son, Nate beamed with pride as he shared that Michael never missed a team chapel, and the leadership role Michael played with the Hawks.

He talked of Michael's ability to keep the team loose when needed, and bragged about Michael's penchant for playing his best in the biggest moments.

"We had a tradition at Heartland to pull guys together early in the season and ask them to share with the team their biggest fear. It's a way to get to know each other and bond as a team."

"Michael stood up and told us how his Mom and Dad made sure he never wanted for anything, how they always made sure he had the best equipment and everything he needed. He told the team my biggest fear is I will not be able to provide for my kids the way my Mom and Dad provided for me."

There wasn't a dry eye in the house. Through tears, Metzger added "that made an impact on me, and I know it impacted several players as well."

He paused as video of the glorious home run Michael hit in the 2012 Junior College World Series was played on the massive video screens.

Coach Metzger then explained baseball "walk-up" songs – music specifically chosen by baseball players to blare over stadium sound systems at games to accompany their walk from the dugout to home plate for each at bat.

"Michael made a statement with his walk-up song," Nate said. "And we would like to play that song one more time for Michael."

As he sat down, Michael's favorite walk-up song faded in: "Saved the Day" by Phillips, Craig and Dean.

> *Rescued from the shackles of my failure*
> *In the dead of night, You shined Your light*
> *Your gift of love is hope that springs eternal*
> *And because of You, all things are new*
> *You saved the day*
> *You tore the holy veil away*
> *You opened wide the prison gates*
> *You saved the day…*

Gift of Hope presented us with various items to commemorate Michael's generous act of organ donation: the flag Jimmy raised at the hospital the day Michael passed; a beautiful bronze medallion for display; and most importantly, a folder documenting the impacts of Michael's selfless decision.

His liver, pancreas and kidneys restored new life. His donated tissue offers improved quality of life for hundreds of recipients. His corneas restored sight to a blind woman in New York.

Representatives from the Exercise Science department at Illinois State University presented Kelly and me with Michael's diploma.

He was so proud of his work at ISU, and had told us he definitely planned on walking across the stage at the graduation ceremony in May.

Then another song was played. Michael was a big Luke Bryan fan, and our family had quickly latched on to the anthem Luke Bryan had written after the death of his brother.

> *Sometimes the greater plan*
> *Is kinda hard to understand*
> *Right now it don't make sense*
> *I can't make it all make sense*
>
> *So I'm gonna sit right here*
> *On the edge of this pier*
> *Watch the sunset disappear*
> *And drink a beer*

Kelly knew a large crowd would gather for this funeral, and she knew the gathering would no doubt include many lost souls and non-believers.

She asked our dear friend and Pastor, Nicki Green, to seize this opportunity by sharing the simple message of the gospel.

Nicki spoke eloquently and passionately; about God and His creation; about the fall as people disobeyed; about rescue, hope and restoration in Jesus Christ.

"You can accept the rescue of God by admitting your needs to God," she told the audience. "Ask Him to forgive you and help you turn from sin, trusting in Jesus alone to rescue you, and making Jesus the Lord of your life today."

She invited anyone wanting to know more to meet her at the cross after the service.

Then Kelly somehow walked up on that stage and delivered an amazing eulogy – a tribute that could only come from a wonderful Christian momma with a deep love for her son, and her Lord Jesus.

As I reflect back starting with the Sunday before the accident, I was blessed with some quality time with Michael that I would like to share with you today.

Sunday, March 23rd – my husband feels that the only furniture you should buy should already come together. However, after purchasing a shelving unit, I needed someone with patience to put it together. After bribing Michael first with Buffalo Wild Wings, he informed me he had to work out then would be right over. Two hours of pure one on one time, stopping only for last second shots of March Madness on TV, the project was complete. Dinner followed with re-runs of Sienfeld while Jeezy, our Pit Bull, was curled up in a ball on the couch next to him.

Monday, March 24th – My oldest son Jimmy and his girlfriend Abby were moving into a new home. Once again, I asked Michael to come over to help me load some furniture and help deliver it to them. After arriving, Jimmy needed additional help and Michael immediately agreed. He met several members of Abby's family, scored a pizza from Papa Johns, and headed to practice with his Dad.

Wednesday, March 26th – I don't know why, but in four years of college, only one other time did I ask him to go grocery shopping. While shopping at Meijers, I lost track of him for one minute. Wondering where he was, he rounded the corner balancing an armful of lunch-ables, chips and cookies. He could not pile it in the cart fast enough – while flashing that beautiful smile. Then the next day I received this text:

"Thanks again for taking me shopping. It's nice to have food around here and I had a great time with you! Nothing like a good day of momma bear and baby bear bonding."

Friday, March 29th – Michael was attending a semi-formal that evening at ISU. At 7:30 I received a picture of him all dressed up making a face. The message with the picture said – "Leonardo Dicaprio or MC? My hair looks great."

I immediately told him I liked his hair short. Then after a few more exchanges my last contact came at 11:18 and it was a picture of him and his date. And for the record – his hair was looking great!

I've seen countless signs and wonders, and people have shared with me their own experiences. I quote, "Signs and wonders do not always indicate the intimate presence of God. On an intimate level God is more likely to come to us in stillness and quiet. And since He neither shouts nor always makes a grand entrance, our alertness becomes crucial."

We weren't looking for signs, at least not from the start, but immediately my son Jimmy noticed the Emergency Room nurse who would be attending Michael in the Operating Room was named James, wore a Bears bandana and had tattoos – which my son Jimmy appreciated! The next day James made the connection that I knew his Mom. We had worked together at Hearts at Home.

Only God…

What followed from the moment he was taken to ICU was so overwhelming that I knew only God could orchestrate these details.

From the head of the Critical Care Unit, to Michael's nurse the first couple days, the ties to multiple families were astounding.

Please allow me to share some other signs that I knew

…Only God.

One evening as I was rushing to get back with Michael, out of the hospital come three therapy dogs. One of them was a huge Pit Bull. If that wasn't enough to make me shake my head, because as most of you know our pit is not a great ambassador for his breed, I asked his name. The owner said Justice, the same legal name as ours. Michael nicknamed him Justice Jamarcus…

Only God…

Next, I would like to show you a picture of our newest family member Maddyn. She was born to Adam and his wife Kacy. On bended knee, my precious nephew held my hand and said they would like to middle name her after Michael. So I present to you Maddyn Ann-Michael Stark

A photo of our newest niece drew sighs and ahs as it appeared on the video screens.

From the time I arrived to the hospital until we released Michael into God's care the song "How Great Thou Art" kept replaying in my mind. "I see the stars, I hear the rolling thunder"…before praying over Michael one final time, our precious Pastor led us in singing that hymn. A couple hours after he passed, I hear the most beautiful sound of rolling thunder…

Only God…

As Jim and I were leaving the floor Thursday morning, a woman I hadn't seen in 35 years approached me. She handed me a note with her phone number as she explained she just lost her 22 year old son six months ago in Afghanistan and she was visiting her father at the hospital.

Only God…

As we were loading up the car to leave BroMenn hospital for the final time Thursday morning, I received a text from Jim's brother, Jeff. He wanted us to know Michael was mentioned in todays edition of The Daily Pantagraph "Pages Past" section. The section summarized a story from five years ago, noting that Michael had a pitching win that day.

Only God…

After meeting with Eastview's funeral coordinator, she grabs my hand and says "Thank You" for Michael being an organ donor – my daughter is a recipient of heart valves.

Only God…

A few days ago I received a text from Tawni Ricketts who is recovering in Iowa from a fractured pelvis and spine injury as a result of the accident. It reads…

"I just wanted to let you know I'm thinking of you and your family and sending you lots of love. Yesterday, my mom and sister were shopping for some loose clothing for me that would be comfy in a wheelchair. They sent me this picture.

A picture of a large mirror in the display window of a store was shown on the giant screens at the front of the sanctuary. The initials "MC" were in one corner of the mirror.

"They said this was a random mirror sitting in the window of an unoccupied store. We see and feel Michael everywhere. Love you!"

Only God...

Lastly, my sweet friend Nicki offered to take me clothes shopping last Saturday. Now I'm sure she had NO idea what she was getting into since I hate malls and shopping. Michael also knew my dislike for the whole mall experience. As we stepped in the front doors I took approximately 10 steps and stopped cold.

Another picture filled the giant sanctuary screens. It was two shirts side by side in the large storefront window. Two simple words adorned the front of each shirt. The first one said "Momma Bear." The one next to it said "Baby Bear."

"A storefront had these hanging in their window."

Only God...

Lastly, as my husband and I pulled into the church yesterday afternoon for the visitation, the song "Blessings" played on WCIC. Michael loved that song. And all the people said...

Only God…

God is present. He has never left me nor forsaken me throughout this whole nightmare. We can choose to be bitter or better. But it is a choice. I'm choosing to be better because let me stress for all of you here, no one will destroy my faith in Christ and I will continue to give God the glory until I draw my last breath.

So many of you have commented repeatedly on my strength over the past several days. Please understand it's not me, it's all from God. In 2 Corinthians 12 Paul writes, "Three different times I begged the Lord to take it away. Each time he said, 'My grace is all you need. My power works best in weakness.' For when I am weak, then I am strong."

The Gift of Hope representative had it right. After completing the questionnaire she looked up and said "Wow, what an awesome kid." I explained I typically reserve that word for God only, but I felt it was time to make an exception.

I would like to close with what Dr. Ginzburg wrote in the comment section of a fund-raising campaign his family contributed to.

"I never knew Michael in life but I had the privilege and sadness of witnessing his passing. I know that has made me a better person and I think the world is a better place just for the brief time Michael was here."

"I know your hearts are heavy at this time. However, try to take comfort in the fact that Michael lives on, not just in the people whose lives will be saved by his ultimate donation, but also in the hearts of everyone he has touched during his life and at his very untimely death."

"With love, Dr. Alan Ginzburg and family."

It can't be said better than that.

Now I will have Michael's brother Jimmy, his girlfriend Abby and some of Michael's cousins come up and read from the "Jesus Calling" devotional. I gifted this to my niece, Sara, not long ago when she was going through a difficult time, and I thank God she remembered to bring it. At one of my lowest points she came to me and read an entry about trusting. Each day family members would take turns reading to Michael.

Thank you for your gift of time to our family. We love you all.

We heard many wonderful compliments about the service from many friends, family, and acquaintances in attendance. One of the most meaningful acknowledgements came from Ryan Knox.

Ryan was an assistant coach at Heartland the two years Michael played for the Hawks. Michael loved coach Knox – even when he pushed him hard in practice to get better. They became even better friends after Michael left Heartland. They both loved the game of golf and spent many days together on a variety of Central Illinois courses over the last two years.

We were aware Coach Knox had grown up in the Catholic church, but we were also aware he had struggled at times with his faith. He approached Kelly and me after the services.

"I've only felt the real presence of God three times in my life," Coach Knox said through a lump in his throat and forming tears. "The first was when my son Owen was born. The second was the day my daughter Chloe was born," he added.

"The third one was today."

Only God…

CHAPTER 19

• • • • • • •

Community = One Team

The twin cities of Bloomington-Normal is a college community boasting a combined population of nearly 100,000 when counting the approximately 20,000 students on campus at Illinois State University nine months of the year.

Measured in restaurants per capita it is a large, metropolitan city. Measured in most other ways that mean anything, it is still a small town.

It certainly wasn't by choice, but the events surrounding Michael's death played out in a very, very public way.

The fact Michael was so young and had achieved some notoriety, as a baseball player at Normal West High School and Heartland Community College, was one factor.

My position as head coach at University High School and some of the publicity I had garnered locally during my days playing fastpitch softball were a part of it.

But the biggest factor was the sordid and horrifying details of the crash and the terrible decisions the drunk driver made before, during, and after.

For weeks and months it seemed like hardly a day could pass without something related to these tragic events finding their way into any and all media outlets.

It was everywhere we turned.

The Daily Pantagraph newspaper is still the primary source of news in Bloomington-Normal. Everyone in the community was talking about this tragedy.

Daily updates and storylines about the circumstances that had the community buzzing helped sell papers and on-line subscriptions.

A reporter was assigned to the on-going investigation, and she seemed to find something to report on daily. Crash details as they continued to unfold; details of the on-going investigation; the passenger in the car that struck Michael claiming a third person had been driving but fled the scene; the subsequent arrest of that passenger on obstruction of justice charges; the arrest of the drunk driver; the not-guilty plea from the drunk driver; the subsequent guilty plea from the drunk driver after confirmation that it was her DNA all over the driver side air bag.

The barrage of publicity wasn't limited to details of the crash and investigative work that followed, and it certainly wasn't limited to the Daily Pantagraph. All the local media outlets followed the story. The local radio stations, led by WJBC, followed in lockstep with the Daily Pantagraph in their on-going and daily barrage of coverage.

Television stations covering the Bloomington-Normal area found ways to keep the story fresh. It was everywhere. Video from the visitation and funeral; pictures and video from the makeshift memorial at the crash site, which grew daily; mug shots following arrests of the driver and passenger; pictures and details from the courtroom when the defendants and our family appeared in court.

To be fair, the media also covered the many wonderful and

heart-warming tributes taking place around the community in honor and memory of Michael.

*** Friends first, Rivals second ***

A few days after the funeral, our U-High baseball team was scheduled to play our archrival, the Central Catholic Saints. The intense rivalry between the schools had existed for decades across all sports, with the two schools in the same city competing together in the same Corn Belt Conference.

On this night, the rivalry would be put aside.

In a touching tribute to Michael, and a heartfelt acknowledgement of what our U-High program was going through, the Central Catholic team did not wear their standard blue and gold game jerseys.

Instead, every single Central Catholic player wore a black shirt with "We Stand With U" on the front.

The "U" was even our trademark University High logo.

And every single jersey was Michael's number 19.

Both teams gathered at second base for a prayer before the game.

I wasn't there to see it – but when our team presented me with a poster signed by seemingly every student at Central Catholic, it was clear what an impact this kind and loving gesture from our rivals had made on our players.

The other Bloomington-Normal high schools joined in the tributes and show of support.

When the baseball teams from Normal West and Normal Community squared off neither team wore its standard game jersey, donning instead newly-made shirts with "MCstrong" on the front, and all with number 19 on the back.

Bloomington High School would do the same in a contest against our U-High team a couple weeks later.

*** *Heartland jersey retirement* ***

Heartland Community College home baseball games are played at the Corn Crib, a 6,000 seat all-turf stadium which is also home to the Normal CornBelters, an independent professional baseball team. A typical Heartland home game would attract maybe 40 or 50 fans – mostly parents of players.

On a gorgeous, sun-drenched Sunday afternoon not long after the funeral, hundreds of people showed up at the Corn Crib for a Heartland baseball game.

The fans weren't really there to watch baseball though.

They were there to watch Heartland retire Michael's number 19 jersey as part of a pregame ceremony.

The bright green artificial turf was basked in glorious sun with nary a cloud in the sky.

Michael wouldn't have it any other way.

A large sign "In Memory of Michael Collins" with the Heartland Hawk logo and #19 was unveiled, to proudly hang on the outfield wall at all Heartland home games.

A giant "MC 19" was meticulously stenciled in bright white paint against the plush green turf behind home plate.

Coach Metzger presented us with Michael's "home white" number 19 Hawks jersey, mounted in a one-of-a-kind, handcrafted walnut case with a glass front. He then took the microphone to pay tribute to his fallen player.

"In his two years at Heartland, Michael was everything we could want and expect an athlete to be. Michael had the unique ability to put a smile on everyone's face. He was quick-witted with a joke, and he was as tough a competitor as anyone we've ever seen at Heartland. No one cared more for his teammates and no one wanted to win more than MC did."

Trying to choke back tears, Metzger continued. "When something like this happens, all the cliché things are thrown around like 'He was a great kid. He was a smart kid. He was liked by everybody.' But with Michael, it's not cliché. That was him."

The hundreds gathered stood and cheered in unison as the home run Michael hit in the 2012 Junior College World Series was replayed on the giant scoreboard in right field.

They all stood again as the outfield banner was unveiled and the glass-cased jersey was presented to us.

And right behind the backstop, standing as one team, were players and parents from the U-High baseball program.

*** *Michael Collins Night – The Normal Cornbelters* ***

Normal CornBelters president and general manager Steve Malliet is a good Christian man and had been following Michael's story. He knew how much Michael enjoyed playing at the Corn Crib. He worked through Coach Metzger to ask if we would like to have a "Michael Collins Night" at the Corn Crib.

We said, "yes" – and God started orchestrating the details.

On an ordinary night the CornBelters draw somewhere south of 1,000 people for a home game.

Not on Michael Collins night.

One of the largest crowds of the season came out to pay tribute to our fallen hero and his family.

Marketing is at the core of any minor league baseball organization, and the creative souls in the CornBelters front office came up with the idea of dedicating a seat in the stadium to honor Michael.

All of the 3,000 chair-back seats in the Corn Crib are green. A single green seat right behind the third base dugout was removed, replaced by a Heartland navy blue chair with Michael's name on it. The 'Belters pledged never to sell that seat for any event.

Michael would always have the "best seat in the house."

Some dear family friends had offered us a generous donation for some kind of memorial tribute if we were interested. They were thinking a memorial bench, or plaque and tree combination, placed somewhere locally for our family to enjoy.

God – or maybe it was Michael – placed a different plan in my heart.

Michael loved baseball and he loved playing at the Corn Crib. We ordered a large, bronze plaque just like the ones found at the baseball Hall of Fame museum in Cooperstown. The CornBelters allowed us to hang the beautiful bronze tribute to our precious son just outside the main entrance gate.

He will always have a presence at the place he loved so much.

Pat McKenna was the CornBelters shortstop. He had worked out some with Michael and the Hawks the last couple springs during Heartland practices. Pat approached GM Steve Malliet and asked if all the CornBelters could wear number 19 in honor of Michael.

The CornBelters official colors are green and gold. But on this night they wore the navy blue and silver of Heartland. The jerseys were emblazoned with "MCstrong" on the front.

And every player on the field wore number 19.

Larry and Vivian Lefferts live in Lincoln, Illinois. They lost their son John to a brain aneurysm. Like Michael, John was an organ donor. We met Larry and Vivian through the Gift of Hope.

What we didn't know was they own a company that makes fireworks, and supply the Cornbelters on "Fireworks Night," which always attracts additional families to the ballpark. As soon as Larry and

Vivian caught wind of a plan for "Michael Collins Night" at the Corn Crib, they donated fireworks for the evening.

The fireworks were matched with several of Michael's favorite songs. Through many tears, our family watched together in a private box and thought of Michael as his special songs played and fireworks lit up the sky.

It was a special end to a special evening.

*** ISU / Secretary of State Ceremony ***

A few short days later, our family gathered again on the campus of Illinois State University for another special ceremony.

Illinois Secretary of State Jesse White presented us with a framed commemorative license plate bearing Michael's initials to recognize the commitment Michael made to the organ donor program.

"As an organ donor, Michael's donation has led to the improvement of 200 people's lives," White said. He turned to Kelly and me and added, "What a tremendous gift. I want to applaud, commend and thank you for bringing into this world this fine young man."

Illinois State University President Larry Dietz also had a gift for us – a beautifully matted and framed Illinois State University diploma Michael had earned.

"It's a token of our gratitude. Michael was, and will always be, a part of our larger Illinois State University family," Dietz said.

The tributes were uplifting in such a desperate time of grief and pain, but God had even more and bigger plans to bring joy out of such a senseless tragedy.

The best was yet to come.

CHAPTER 20

● ● ● ● ● ● ● ●

Pay It Forward – #MCstrong

Hailey Lanier and Michael went separate ways following the dance on March 28th, and Hailey was not in the car when Michael was killed. Devastated by the loss of her friend, Hailey created an event page on Facebook titled "Pay It Forward for Michael Collins."

The idea was simple – friends and family could honor Michael through random acts of kindness and share those acts on the Facebook page.

It was simply intended to be a way for family and friends to deal with their pain and grief, and for something good to come from such a senseless tragedy.

It became obvious rather quickly that God had bigger plans.

It started as expected, with friends, family and acquaintances around the Bloomington-Normal community sharing their acts.

"I had been waiting for NWHS's prom to walk into a restaurant and pick a prom couple to buy their dinner. I was too emotional to get

many words out but I think they felt the love for Michael! He seemed to love a good prom!"
Pam Fisher Cullen – Facebook post https://www.facebook.com/ events/247105598806537/)

"Today i go back to work after an amazing summer break!!!! We were able to spend most of our summer doing what we love....watching Sean play the game he's so passionate about....baseball. Yesterday was the last 2014 summer break day we would be able to spend together as a family. What did we do? Thanks to Brian Read, we spent the day at Wrigley Field. 3 months ago when Brian found out that Sean had never been to an MLB game he walked up to me, hands me Cub tickets and said "I'd like to pay it forward in the name of Michael Collins, take Sean to this game". What an amazing gesture!!!! The look on Sean's face when we walked into Wrigley Field for batting practice was priceless!!! What an amazing way to end the summer!! Once again, thank you Brian Read"
Cheryl Morris Shook – Facebook post https://www.facebook. com/events/247105598806537/

"My 12 year old son wanted to donate his $15 that he made from his lemonade sale to St.Judes and when I told him I needed to find out where to send it he said drop it off at the building next to State Farm in town...after driving by & him pointing out the sign where it said "MCstrong." I realized he meant OSF St. Joseph Medical Center. He wanted it to go to the Michael Collins foundation. This story has touched so many lives..including my 12 year old son! Continued prayers for The Michael Collins Family! God Bless!"
Brenda "Foor" Banter – Facebook post https://www.facebook. com/events/247105598806537/

"I've been wanting to pay it forward in honor of Michael Collins, but have been waiting until it felt like the right moment. I finally had that moment today. My son and I went to his doctor appointment and as we were visiting with the doctor she mentioned to me that she is trying to find funding for some of her pediatric patients who do not have the money to pay for their therapy supplies. She said the families of some of her patients have trouble finding the money to buy gas to get

to the kids' appointments, let alone having money to buy the supplies they need for their therapy. I asked her how many of her patients are in that situation right now. She said there is only one child at this time, but she never knows when she'll have others. The little boy is 10 years old and his condition causes him to have embarrassing moments in front of his peers. His parents are divorced and he is in his dad's custody, but his dad is not healthy. His grandparents are trying to do the best they can for him and his younger brother, but they don't have the money for the supplies he needs to help resolve his condition. It was clear that this was our moment to pay it forward. I told her we would pay for his supplies. Did I plan to spend this money today? No. Would I like to keep it for our family? Sure. Will our family survive without it? Yes. A small sacrifice for our family is an impossibility for another family. There was no way I could leave her office knowing there is a little boy in this sad situation and I could have helped him, but chose not to. After the appointment my son said to me, "I haven't seen you cry in a long time." I told him those were tears of sadness for this boy's situation and tears of happiness that God put us where we needed to be today so we could help him. Thank you Michael Collins for being an inspiration. And thank you to Michael's parents for raising such an inspiring young man."

Tiffany Runyon Giganti – Facebook post https://www.facebook.com/events/247105598806537/

"I completed #10 of my pledge to do 19 acts of paying it forward for Michael. Mowed my neighbors yard because he has been battling pancreatic problems."

Jeff Paul – Facebook post https://www.facebook.com/events/247105598806537/

"My mom bought tickets for a Keith Urban concert that was last weekend. She realized she couldn't go and decided that instead of selling the tickets she would give them away to honor Michael. She found someone on Craigslist that seemed like they would appreciate them and pay it forward. Just seeing this little girls sweet face and hearing how much she enjoyed the concert is the little things in life that brings us joy! #MCStrong forever and always. Miss you Mike."

Erin Huddleston – Facebook post https://www.facebook.com/events/247105598806537/

"Love this and had to share. My cousin Marcie makes stuffed bears for the Mother Bear Project. These bears bring comfort to children affected by AIDS. The children often call their bear by the name on the tag. This bear, in U-High colors, is named Michael, and was made in honor of MC. Here's a picture of this special bear with his young recipient in Lesotho, South Africa."
Susan Rink – Facebook post https://www.facebook.com/events/247105598806537/

Then we started seeing these acts of kindness posted from various other communities throughout the state of Illinois.

"As of yesterday I did not know who Michael Collins was or anything about him. That all changed last night. My son plays for a traveling baseball team & after their tournament the boys & parents went to La Casa Mexicana in Edwardsville, IL. After we were seated, the waiter came to us all & gave us a note & said he had cheese dip & guacamole for everyone from someone in honor of Michael Collins. I can not even begin to tell you how much impact the note had on all of us! And the gift of goodies was awesome too! Thanks to whoever you were because you touched our hearts. Our boys will be paying it forward in honor of Michael very soon!"
(This post was accompanied with a picture of a note that was left. It read:
Boys: Never give up on your dreams and always remember to play from the heart!
Signed: In honor of Michael Collins #MCstrong #PayItForward
Lori Napier Blackburn (Edwardsville, IL) – Facebook post https://www.facebook.com/events/247105598806537/

"This week, as an office, we'll be looking for ways to Pay It Forward in honor of Michael Collins, a senior at Illinois State University who recently passed away after being hit by a drunk driver-but because he was a donor, over 200 people were helped due to organ and tissue

donation. As a part of the Pay It Forward movement, we encourage you to find a way to pay it forward to someone else today, too. Big or small, it all adds up and makes a difference. In honor of Michael...
#mcstrong"
Katie Young (Lincoln, IL) – Facebook post https://www.facebook.com/events/247105598806537/

Then the most amazing thing happened. Posts started popping up in different states! Some of the posts were from friends, friends of friends, family, and friends of family as they traveled in the U.S. Others were strangers who knew somebody impacted, or strangers who heard from somebody about the tragedy and the Pay It Forward movement.

"Being thankful for the MCStrong pay it forward opportunity my mom received, she and I decided to pay it forward in New York. On the last day, at the right place, at the right time, waiting for the train to arrive, my mom noticed a lady getting out of a car. As their eyes met, she had a big smile, several times. My mom had thought to herself, this is it... I am going to buy her train ticket. We all entered the elevator together. We walked in the same direction but somehow we lost her. She was already in the process of paying for her ticket. We went over to her and overheard her tell her mom she had tried to buy a ticket several times but her credit card would not work. We offered to buy her train ticket and right away her eyes were teary. I explained the MCStrong movement and told her about Michael. She said she was visiting her mom and buying a wedding dress. She immediately said that she was planning to pay it forward- her plan is to donate her wedding dress after her big day! The four of us, 2 moms and 2 daughters with tears in our eyes began to exchange bits of info. We are from Bloomington, they are from Bloomingdale. As Collins is Michael's last name, they lived on Collins St. It was all meant to be! #MCstrong"
Alyson Packheiser (New York City) – Facebook post https://www.facebook.com/events/247105598806537/

"Paying it forward #MCStrong in Richardson, TX! This young man's father, a dear family friend was killed in a motorcycle accident around the same time as the loss of Michael. He's hoping to help his family out as well as earn some spending money by mowing lawns this summer. In the spirit of Michael Collins and paying it forward he now has a new lawn mower! Don't Drink and Drive and God Bless the Collins Family!"
Mark Young (Richardson, TX) – Facebook post https://www.facebook.com/events/247105598806537/

"So on the last day of a 4 day music festival I went to in Rothbury, MI called Electric Forest I decided to wear my custom neon yellow MCstrong shirt to take Michael Collins to the forest. That night I decided I was going to conquer my fear of heights by standing on the Ferris wheel. While waiting in line of about 100 people for the Ferris wheel debating whether the line was too long or not we decided we had to ride it on the last night for the last concert. While in line a couple came up to my friends and I and asked if anyone can give them $5 cause they didn't have enough cash for both of them to ride it. When I checked and saw I had enough, I gave them the money and told them to have a great rest of the forest. Without even thinking of the pay it forward movement and the fact that I was wearing my MCstrong shirt for the first time. When I realized a few minutes later, I told them I didn't mean to be a buzz kill on the good vibes before the Ferris wheel but needed to tell them Michael's story since I was wearing his shirt. I told them the story and it couldn't have happened at a more natural point. I conquered my fear of heights and stood up on the moving Ferris wheel that night so thank you Michael."
Dee Sanetra (Rothbury, MI) – Facebook post https://www.facebook.com/events/247105598806537/

"#MCStrong is alive in Fargo, ND. Just paid athletic fees for a student/athlete so he can play football and basketball."
Marybeth Drendel Althoff (Fargo, ND) – Facebook post https://www.facebook.com/events/247105598806537/

"Today I got to share Michael's story with my OT class at Indiana State. I had to do a presentation about myself and bring one thing

with me that I always have. Every day I wear my bracelet in honor of MC that says "Hawks Fly Together #19" for our Heartland family. After my presentation, I had a classmate ask what they can do for MC and his foundation. I told them to just spread the word about MC and educate people on drunk driving. It's so great to know I'm surrounded by such caring people and to know Michael's story will continue to be passed on.
#MCstrong"
Jessica Toth (Terre Haute, Indiana) – Facebook post https://www. facebook.com/events/247105598806537/

"I'm sure I'm with everyone else that today has brought many tears being Michael's birthday. After a rough morning of tears, I went and sat on the beach. I prayed that Michael would send me a sign letting me know he is doing good up there in Heaven. Not a few minutes later, a single rose washed up at my feet. Just wanted to let everyone know he is doing well. I figured he would want me to share his message."
Brandi Tucker (Miramar Beach, Florida) – Facebook post https:// www.facebook.com/events/247105598806537/

And if there was any doubt at this point God was at work, we started seeing "Pay It Forward for Michael Collins" posts all around the world!

"I am in Dublin, Ireland leading a group of ISU students on study abroad. I have been thinking about a pay it forward to honor Michael in Dublin especially since I am with students. Today it also happens to be my wedding anniversary, I was going to do it today as way to celebrate my 19 year marriage and my two boys, one who goes to West, but I was having a hard time planning the logistics. When I saw that it was also Michael's birthday today I knew I had to do it. As I was quietly eating a celebratory dinner by myself, an American couple came in next to me and asked to split the single diners special. As I was explaining to the waitress what this was all about I was suddenly overcome with such emotion that I had to leave quickly. Pay It Forward, Dublin, Ireland, May 20, 2014."

Carrie Anna Courtad (Dublin, Ireland) – Facebook post https:// www.facebook.com/events/247105598806537/

"A high school friend of mine started my Saturday off with this one and I had to share. Thank you Robert Hinshaw! MCStrong being shared in Ecuador and part of a Bible Study to boot. Here was the Message from Bob…….
"Jeff, I wanted to pass this picture to you from Pueblo Viejo, Ecuador just a few miles from Alausi, Ecuador. We shared Michael's story with the kids of the village as a part of our Bible study. We passed out the MC Strong bracelets. The kids loved them and were wearing them the whole time we were there."
Jeff Collins (Ecuador) – Facebook post https://www.facebook. com/events/247105598806537/

"My husband and I are from Le Roy, Illinois and now we are living and serving in the Dominican Republic. When we learned about Michael and his family along with millions of others….our hearts broke. We didn't personally know the Collin's family but we love many people that know and love them. Being parents of 5 children we cannot comprehend what the Collin's family is feeling. As missionaries we speak to people about eternity and we know our sole purpose of being on this planet is to live by Jesus' example, love people with your whole heart, help others and most importantly lead people to Christ. Michael has inspired so many people with his actions and his leadership. One area we serve is a village named Munoz. Munoz is home to mostly people from Haiti that came to the DR for a better life. This is an area that lives on hope, kindness and God's promises. We shared with them today about Michael and the importance of how our actions affect others. I won't soon forget their faces as they listened about the legacy that Michael has left. One by one during the game, they would come over and just hold his photo. He will now be a role model for these beautiful children too. Thank you Collin's family for accomplishing what all us parents hope to do….raise a child that is a world changer! ~ Jenny and Brian Bland.
With a Pay It Forward donation we were able to purchase more equipment for our softball ministry with Go MAD Ministries. Go

MAD means "Go Make A Difference! Thank you Michael for making a difference! #mcstrong #mcfuerte"
Jenny Bland – Facebook post https://www.facebook.com/events/247105598806537/

But God wasn't finished. As if we weren't humbled enough by this outpouring of support, now the story took an even more amazing turn!

Somebody at Sports Illustrated had picked up on this Pay It Forward phenomenon going viral and the random deeds being done around the globe in honor of Michael. They wanted to do a story!

Our Michael would grace the pages of the iconic and beloved sports magazine!

I took a phone call, answered a few questions, and then waited anxiously.

And then it arrived. The May 19th issue.

Yes, the 19th!

You can look it up.

May 19, 2014 issue – page 16.

Two pictures of our precious son; one in his Heartland Hawk baseball uniform and another in a nice shirt and sweater, flashing that million-dollar smile for the world to see. On the same page as legendary football coach Bill Belichick!

The accompanying story was neatly placed between the two photos.

Positive Influence
Good deeds follow the death of a player and coach

The article mentioned gestures like a $70 tip on a $90 restaurant bill, and somebody paying for a kid to go to a baseball camp. It referenced random acts of kindness in 46 states and 15 countries, all appearing on the "Pay it Forward for Michael Collins" page on Facebook and featuring the hashtag #MCstrong – and all in the name of Michael. The short but touching tribute mentioned Michael's work as a volunteer assistant coach at University High School, and his decision to be an organ donor.

In the several months prior to Michael's death, Johnny Manziel was becoming famous as a quarterback at Texas A&M, and for flashing his "money" sign when he scored a touchdown.

This signature move caught on with Michael, and he would often be seen in pictures imitating the "money" sign.

Manziel was drafted by the Cleveland Browns, and was on the front cover of this May 19th issue!

Michael wore number 19 from his very first days in travel baseball as a 10 year old. Normal West retired his #19 jersey. Heartland Community College retired his #19 jersey.

The Sports Illustrated article appeared in the May 19th edition.

It was one day before Michael's birthday.

Only God indeed.

CHAPTER 21

· · ● ● ● ● ● ● ·

There is No Playbook

On Thursday, April 9, the Pioneers lost another conference game to archrival Central Catholic, 7-2. The loss put our overall record at 1-3, and dropped our conference mark to 1-2. It was certainly not the start our players, or coaches, had envisioned.

But so far, what about this season had been anything any of us could have imagined? Still, Assistant Coach Steve Paxson, as the man currently in charge, was struggling with the slow start.

"I am not used to losing this many games," Coach Paxson lamented to me in a phone call following the Central Catholic loss. Coach Paxson had been very successful for 10 years as head coach at Brimfield High School, a tiny community just west of Peoria.

"Our hitters are pathetic," Coach Paxson moaned. "They are taking good pitches early in the count and then chasing bad pitches when they get in the hole. Our infielders are kicking the ball all over the place. I've been getting after them pretty good in practice. They need to focus."

Coach Paxson was our pitching coach, so it didn't necessarily surprise me when hitting and defense were the primary problems he mentioned. I did gently remind him we had allowed seven runs or more in three of the games, so our pitchers were struggling some too.

But at this point, I really wasn't concerned about any of it. My concern was with our guys.

"Coach," I said, "we have to cut 'em some slack. These guys have been through something no high school kids should ever have to go through. They had to go in a room, hold Michael's hand, and tell him goodbye. They went to a funeral and visitation of an assistant coach only a couple years older than they are. An assistant coach they loved. I don't expect them to be focused on baseball."

"I know," Coach Paxson sighed. "It's been tough on all of us. The boys loved Michael. They love you. And they are worried about you."

I didn't think I was ready to come back and coach, but I decided I at least owed my team a conversation.

I found out some parents were going to purchase enough "Ringers" (remember the special burger Michael and some of the boys had created at Meatheads) and french fries to feed the team and coaching staff after practice on Friday. Just the mention of "The Ringer" made me start to cry, but I decided that would be a good day for me to visit practice and address the team.

I arrived at Redbird Field as practice was nearing completion. Just pulling into the parking lot put a knot in my stomach and a lump in my throat. It would be my first time with the team, at this place, without Michael.

It was a beautiful spring day. The green of the infield turf seemed to pop and sparkle in the sunlight, and the lack of a typical central Illinois spring breeze made the afternoon feel even warmer than the 70 degrees on the thermometer.

I can't explain why, but I was terribly nervous. It felt like I was meeting the players and coaches for the first time. The players were cleaning up after practice. Bruce and Wendy Auer were the first people I saw. They were setting up dinner on the stadium concourse. They were parents of Travis, a senior pitcher, and long-time friends of my family. Travis was very close to Michael. Tears filled in their eyes as I gave each of them a hug. They both wanted to talk, but the tears wouldn't let them. "The boys are going to be so glad to see you," Wendy managed, her voice trembling.

I slowly walked down the steps toward the dugout.

The players and coaches were settled onto the bleachers behind our dugout. A few parents who had been there to serve dinner stood at the railing directly behind the players. I stood in front of the first row of bleachers, looking at them.

I looked into their eyes. Several of them had tears forming. I started to speak, but my lips started quivering and my eyes filled with tears. I looked away.

I took a deep breath, and decided to push forward.

"Gentlemen," I started. "I have been coaching a long time. I have hundreds of books about leadership on my bookshelves at home. None of them tell me what I am supposed to do or how I am supposed to act in this situation."

"So I am just going to do what I have always tried to do with you guys, and that is to be truthful. I'm just going to share my feelings with you, and see if somehow we can get through this together."

I didn't really know how to address the question I was certain they wanted answered. "I don't know when, or even if, I will come back to coach," I said. "I just know I'm not ready right now."

"Michael loved you guys and he loved his Dad, and I know he would want me to get back out here and be with you guys," I continued through sobs. "But I also know how much he loved his Mom, and I need to make sure she is okay being alone before I start leaving her for practices and games."

I paused for a moment, attempting to gather myself. "I believe in God, and Michael did too. I miss him terribly. But to believe in God is to believe Michael is in a better place. That is what keeps me going."

I held up a copy of Tony Dungy's book.

"When Michael was a junior in high school, I led a book study for baseball players at Normal West' I recalled. "We studied this book – Dare to be Uncommon. As an assignment during the study I asked the players to write their own obituary. I still have the paper Michael wrote. I would like to read it to you."

"Michael was a good kid who enjoyed spending time with friends and family. His favorite sports included baseball, basketball and golf. His hobbies included fishing and other activities. He was a strong believer in Jesus Christ and helped others look to follow God. He enjoyed making people laugh until he died."

"He enjoyed making people laugh until the day he died," I repeated.

By now my eyes just weren't watering, tears actually trickled down my face.

"I have been spending a lot of time asking myself, 'what would Michael want.' I know this fellas – Michael loved baseball and he had fun playing it. He would want you guys to have fun too."

"I haven't been to any of our games so far, but I talk to Coach Paxson every day. I haven't seen a single play but I've heard enough to know you guys aren't having fun. I am giving you permission to have fun. I am telling you Michael would want you to have fun."

"Quit worrying about winning or losing. Quit worrying about hits and errors or how you pitch. I have always told you winning is not the most important thing to me, and I mean that even more now. Just focus on one thing; have fun. For Michael."

"Everybody huddle up," I said. The players got to their feet and gathered together. We raised our hands together as one. "Michael helped create the sandwich we are about to have for dinner. He was so proud of working with you guys on this sandwich. I just know he is smiling down on us tonight."

"Let's enjoy the Ringer and fries tonight," I added. "It's going to be a great day for baseball tomorrow. Relax, enjoy it, and have fun."

"MC on three," I finished. "One, two, three…

"MC!" they yelled in a single voice.

Michael was a middle infielder and pitcher at Normal West High School. He earned all-conference recognition and was selected to play in the Daily Pantagraph and Illinois Coaches Association All-Star games following his senior year. (Photo: Kelly Collins)

Michael played at Heartland Community College in 2011 and 2012. The Hawks advanced to the NJCAA World Series in Enid, OK both years. The Hawks 3rd place finish and Michael's HR in the 2012 World Series was the highlight of his baseball career. (Photo: Kelly Collins)

Michael and Coach Metzger. Michael loved Coach Metz and loved being a Heartland Hawk! (Photo: Kelly Collins)

Michael and I pose with the IHSA State Championship trophy in 2012. Michael was in Enid for the JUCO World Series, but we shared our joyous week during several phone calls. (Photo: Kelly Collins)

Michael was my assistant coach at University High while he attended Illinois State University. Despite a full load of classes, he never missed a game or practice. (Photo: Julianne Mosele)

Michael coaches Nick Mosele at first base. Michael loved Nick. Nick's size and the way he played the game reminded him of a young Michael Collins. (Photo: Julianne Mosele)

The "Pay It Forward" movement reached all the way to the Dominican Republic when some local missionaries shared Michael's story with this group of kids. (Photo: Jenny Bland)

My first game back to coach after Michael's death was against Tri-Valley. The two teams gathered at second base to pray before the game. (Photo: Kristie Galindo)

"MCstrong" started when Michael was in the hospital fighting for his life. It remained the rallying cry to keep our team together throughout the remainder of the 2014 season. (Photo: Julianne Mosele)

A team prayer is the tradition I am most proud of starting while I was head coach at U-High, and Michael inspired me by being in every team prayer when he played at Heartland. (Photo: Kristie Galindo)

Jimmy and I embrace following our exhilarating regional championship win. The watch on my wrist was Michael's – one of the ways I tried to keep him with me during the season. (Photo: Kristie Galindo)

Our seniors host the regional championship trophy! They were an amazing example of overcoming adversity and what can happen when everyone pulls together toward a common goal! (Photo: Kristie Galindo)

I prayed with our seniors following our last game, asking God to use our struggles of tragedy and triumph to light and guide their paths. (Photo: Kristie Galindo)

The team surrounds me after our regional championship win. Based on what they had to endure and how they persevered – the greatest team I've ever coached! (Photo: Kristie Galindo)

PART III
A New Perspective

"And we know that God causes everything to work
together for the good of those who love God and are
called according to His purpose for them"
Romans 8:28

CHAPTER 22

• • • • • • •

Visit with Michael

The following Monday afternoon, I decided it was time for me to go have a talk with Michael. I left work early. Kelly was cleaning up some dishes at the kitchen sink when I walked in the back door.

"I need to go up to the cemetery," I announced, before she even had a chance to ask why I was home so early.

"Do you want me to go with you," she asked.

My voice quivered. "I think I need to go alone, if you don't mind."

She knew I was still in a very dark place. "Okay," she whispered through tears. "Are you sure you will be okay?"

I nodded my head. "I will text you when I get there and text you when I am on the way home," I told her. "I am going to take his truck," I added.

I climbed in his truck, a 2001 Toyota Tundra. He was so proud of his truck. It was the first time I had been in it since his mom and cousin had brought it home to be in our garage.

It used to be my truck. A couple of years ago his Toyota Camry had stopped running, and he convinced me to let him have the Tundra so I could get myself something newer. It didn't take much convincing. He could always talk me into just about anything.

I turned the ignition and stared at the bright display of the stereo system, a system he had added once the truck was "his." He had also added black rims, a sub-woofer for the stereo, and tinted windows. He always talked about getting something bigger and a four-wheel drive, but God how he loved that truck.

I glanced to the back seat. There was the Titleist backpack he used for school. It still had all his textbooks and notebooks in it, just as he had left it the last day he went to class. I looked down at the center console, and saw the "19" sticker he had placed between the two cup holders.

I placed my hand on the steering wheel and stared at the silver ring on my right hand. It had a blue stone in the middle. The outside of the ring said "Diamond Sports World Series Champions." I held my hand up and admired it. The side of the ring I could see was engraved with "18 Gold," reminding me of the summer I coached Michael and his 18U teammates to the championship of the Diamond Sports World Series. It was one of the highlights of our years of baseball together.

I backed down the drive, headed for tiny Gridley, IL and the small, rural cemetery.

The yard sign, one of hundreds the anonymous donor had donated to line the drive of the church for the services, served as a temporary headstone. The wire posts were pushed into the ground so the "19 #MCstrong" strong sign rested on the dirt and grass.

Several flowers of various colors had been placed in front of and behind the sign. Next to the makeshift headstone, held up by a small easel, sat a garden stone. A gift to the family, now being used as a graveside decoration. It read:

"No farewell words
were spoken
No time to say goodbye
You were gone
before we knew it,
and only God knows why"

Just to the right of the sign was a golf ball, placed on a golf tee just visible over the grass. The golf ball was a Titleist Pro V1, Michael's golf ball of choice. "MC 19" was monogrammed on the ball. Autographs from three of his best friends covered the ball. Just days before, they had played a round of golf together in Michael's honor, and all stopped up here to place this ball.

I sat down on the grass. I took another look around to make sure I was alone, and then closed my eyes. I took a deep breath, and started with my regrets.

"Hey buddy, " I started. "I miss you so much."

"I want you know I am sorry for missing so many of your games, for missing your home run at the World Series. I am so sorry I missed your final baseball game."

Just then the stillness was interrupted by a gentle breeze that I felt touch my face.

"Stop," I heard Michael say.

"I was so proud of you winning the state championship! I wouldn't have had it any other way. A lot of the Heartland guys had parents there, but how many could say 'my Dad is coaching in the State Finals'!"

"I know you loved me," he continued.

I sat in stunned silence.

"I remember all the phone calls from you during that week. I knew you were with me in spirit, and I hope you know I was with you in spirit. What a run!"

I remained silent as he continued.

"If only one of us could win I wanted it to be you, and I know you wanted it to be me. That is what made our relationship so special, not whether or not you were actually there."

I finally found the words to speak.

"I don't know how I can go on Michael," I whispered. "It hurts so bad."

"I know Dad," he softly replied.

"It's been an adjustment for me too," he added with a chuckle.

"It took me some time to understand," he continued. "But now I understand the plan. And Dad, I like it here."

God how I miss that smile.

"You need to get back to coaching Dad," he stated.

"I'm just not sure I'm ready for that," I answered. "I am in so much pain. I didn't have a lot of patience before all this, and I'm sure I don't have the patience for all the coaching headaches now."

"Maybe that's part of the plan'" he responded. "Love and patience fit nicely together."

There was that ornery smile again.

"My guys need you," he replied. "You are a great coach and they need you now more than ever."

"You were meant to do it," he added.

"Oh, and Dad? Next time, can you bring your Bible? I like having it read to me."

CHAPTER 23

• • • • • • •

My Return to the Dugout

I had told the team, and others, I couldn't go back to coaching until I knew Kelly would be ok with my time away from home. That was a ruse – she had encouraged me to return to coaching as soon as I was ready. She knew it would be a good distraction from my grief.

My biggest concern was whether or not I had the heart to give our guys the 100% passion and effort they deserved.

I was also concerned about being a distraction. That had become a little less of a concern given our slow start. We had won both games of a Saturday doubleheader following my talk with the team on Friday night, but that was against a weak opponent. We stood at 3-3, had already lost two conference games, and had a tough week ahead. I had become less concerned about my return bringing more bad luck.

I called my Athletic Director, Wendy Smith, on Monday. Wendy and I had our differences during my three years as head coach. We didn't always see eye-to-eye on scheduling issues, bus scheduling and departure times, equipment orders, and the team bonding value of overnight trips.

But as our personal tragedy unfolded, she stepped up to her

leadership role in a very big way, with a level of compassion beyond what I thought existed.

She did everything I would want a leader to do in such horrible, unthinkable circumstances.

She was at the hospital on day one as soon as she got the news, and came to see us every day we were there. She brought in snacks and sandwiches to help feed all the family and friends gathered and holding vigil throughout the days and nights.

She also took care of baseball business. She gathered players and parents early on and provided updates on Michael's condition and conveyed interim plans. She communicated with the other coaches to make sure a plan was in place for practices and games. She worked with other school administrators to make sure the kids had somebody to talk to if needed.

It served as a lesson in service and compassion to get through the most difficult of times – and was such a stark contrast from my boss at my primary place of employment.

I had been through the crash, five horrifically agonizing days in the hospital, Michael's death, visitation and funeral. It was now 12 days since I buried my 22-year- old son. And through it all, I had not heard from this boss. Not a visit. Not a phone call. Not an email. Not a text. Silence. It spoke volumes on the value of compassion in leadership.

And now, Wendy listened as I discussed coming back to coaching and shared some of my trepidations. She stepped up again with all the right responses.

After a few pleasantries, I cut to the chase. "I think I want to make this Saturday my first day back," I said. "That gives me the rest of this week to get ready mentally, and it gets us past a couple of road games this week where Kelly would have to be home by herself."

"You know we would love to have you back Coach," she responded.

"I know the kids miss you. We miss you. But we all want what is best for you."

"If you want to come back Saturday that would be great. If you need a couple more weeks, that's fine too. And if you don't come back at all this spring, I will understand that as well. Whatever you want, we will make it work."

"I am still struggling," I shared. "At times the pain is overwhelming. I don't want to come back and then have to step away because I can't handle it. I don't want to put the kids through that."

"Don't worry about any of that," she replied. "If you come back and then need to take some time off later, that is absolutely not a problem. None of us can imagine what you and Kelly are going through – but everyone will do what we need to help you get through this."

"We will get through this – together," she added.

I was amazingly comforted by the call and her gracious, compassionate response.

I told her I would plan on being there Saturday.

* * *

Then on Wednesday, we won a huge hard-fought battle 2-1 over Intercity rival Normal Community, a 4A school. I had never beaten NCHS as a head coach. On Thursday we avenged an earlier loss against conference foe Eureka in a big way, clobbering the Hornets 14-1 in their home park. And to top the tough week off, the Pioneers went on the road for another conference game against a very good Pontiac team, and came home with a 6-2 victory.

Just like that we had gone from 1-3 to 6-3. And now I was worried about upsetting the apple cart by returning to coach the team.

I talked with Coach Paxson almost every day during my absence from the team. On Friday night, I called him to talk about the win over Pontiac and lineup plans for my return on Saturday.

"Hey Coach," I started. "Another great win tonight."

"Thanks Coach," he said. "The kids are really on a roll right now – really playing well. They are really starting to click."

As if I wasn't concerned enough about disrupting the winning streak!

"You still going to be here tomorrow?" he asked.

"Planning on it," I replied. "I've been playing around with lineups for game one and game two. I would like to have both games pretty much mapped out so I don't have to do a lot of thinking tomorrow. I'm sure it's going to take me awhile to get back in the swing of things."

Different coaches have different philosophies on regular season high school doubleheaders. Some coaches take a "play to win" approach and pretty much put their best lineup on the field for both games. Coaches on the opposite side of the spectrum tend to play their best guys in game one, and a whole new lineup for game two.

I wasn't necessarily on one end of the spectrum or the other, but I have always liked to use doubleheaders to play some guys who might not otherwise get to play.

Tomorrow we would be playing Tri-Valley, a smaller class 2A school. I was thinking it should be a day for all our kids to play one game. Clearly Coach Paxson had some other ideas.

"I'm not saying we can't play a few different kids, but we need to play to win both games and keep this momentum," he offered. "We got different kids an at-bat in the Eureka game," he continued. "I would put our best lineup out there each game. Hopefully we can get a couple big leads tomorrow and then let some other kids play, but let's make sure we get a couple more W's and keep this streak going."

CHAPTER 24

● ● ● ● ● ● ●

MC – Still Coaching

As soon as I hung up from Coach Paxson I started working on lineups for the two games on Saturday.

I sketched two baseball diamonds on a sheet of paper – one for game one and another for game two.

My discussion with Coach Paxson echoed in my head.

I penciled in what I thought to be our best lineup on the game one diamond. I made a couple of tweaks and labeled the other diamond "game two".

I stared at the paper for several minutes. We had 18 players on our roster. Six names didn't appear in either starting lineup.

I pulled out another sheet of paper. I sketched two more diamonds. I wrote the same "best" lineup names for game one. I wrote nine different names for game two. Eighteen players and everybody would start a game.

I spent the next three hours scribbling various combinations of these first two options. Some of the sheets I kept. Other sheets I crumpled and threw away. Around 10:00 pm I gave up and went to bed, hoping it would be clearer by morning.

Sleep had been very elusive since the crash, and it clearly wasn't going to be better tonight. I tossed and turned all night. My confusion and self-doubt over lineups was now escalating to a full blown panic attack that had me wondering if I should be anywhere near a baseball field. The questions were filling my head at a furious pace.

How can I be on that field without Michael?

How can I make decisions when my mind is so clouded?

How will I get through the day without breaking down?

How can I coach when all I can think about is Michael?

I cannot do this…

At 5:30 a.m., a hint of light through the bedroom window suggested the sun was beginning to rise. I thought about texting Wendy and Coach Paxson to tell them I wasn't ready.

I decided to take a walk before contacting them.

Kelly rustled next to me in bed and I whispered that I was going for a walk. I dressed for warmth and headed out our back door and onto our back patio, across from the 18th green at the Ironwood Golf Course. I didn't see any activity yet, but I could hear the faint hum of golf course mowers working in the distance, probably on the first or second hole.

I figured I was less likely to cross paths with any equipment if I walked on the back nine, so I took the cart path around the 18th green and headed up the 10th fairway. The short fairway grass was wet, and as I looked behind me towards the clubhouse I could see my footprints highlighting my path in the early morning dew.

In the middle of this 10th fairway, just past the halfway point of the slight dogleg right, I slowed and then stopped. I was at the 150 yard marker.

This was our spot.

Michael and I would often look out our back window at dusk to see if the 10th hole was clear. If it was, we would each take an iron and play the hole in from this spot. One point for closest to the pin, another point for a birdie, and another point if you won the hole. We would often play the hole and count points well past darkness, when we couldn't tell where the ball landed until we were actually on the green.

I could feel the tears trickling from my eyes.

God I wish I could play this hole with him right now.

At other times for these impromptu evening matches we would play #10, then proceed to #11, then cross the road and play hole 18, with the three-hole match ending right next to our back yard.

I followed the cart path to the tee box on the 11th hole and started down the fairway.

The 11th hole is a picturesque par 5. Picturesque not so much for the beauty of the hole, but for the majestic church steeple and cross in the distance, visible the entire length of the plush 500 yard fairway.

As I saw the steeple and cross in the distance, with the rising sun now shining directly upon it, a slight smile joined the tears.

I recalled some Sunday mornings when Michael would inform us he would not be joining us at church because he would be golfing. He would tell his mom there were times the golf course was his sanctuary, a place of worship.

She couldn't be mad at him when he flashed that smile.

As I looked at the glorious morning rays bouncing off the steeple and cross rising in the sky, it dawned on me he may have been much more serious about being close to God on the golf course than I thought.

I got to the end of the 11th hole and decided to sit down on the bench situated between the green and the next tee box. I closed my eyes and thought about the day ahead, and the lineup decisions I was running out of time to make.

It was a very calm morning, but I felt the slightest hint of a cool breeze touch my face.

"It's about time you got back in the dugout."

Sitting alone on a golf course bench in the glow of early dawn I should have been startled by a voice other than my own. But instead, I felt the strangest calm as I opened my eyes.

Michael was seated next to me. His smile announced he was well aware his presence would make my day.

"What are you doing up so early," he asked.

"Don't you think I should be asking you that question," I retorted. Michael was an early riser only if he had to, and he much preferred a late start.

"I had work to do," he grinned. "Big game today. You ready?"

"I'm struggling with lineup decisions. You know I like to play some different guys in doubleheaders, but I also like to win. And we can use the wins."

"I don't want people to wish I would have stayed home," I added.

"Hey Dad," Michael started. "You remember when we would talk about this and I would always tell you play to win?"

"Yes, that has crossed my mind the last couple days," I answered.

"Well, I was wrong. The two years I played at Heartland, I got a different perspective. I still think winning is important, but it's also important to give guys a chance to play."

I paused. He wasn't finished.

"You have 18 guys on your roster, right?"

I nodded my head yes.

"And we had 18 guys last year, right."

I nodded yes again.

"And the last two years who was probably the 18th man?"

"Probably Parker," I replied.

"And who was the first player at the hospital to greet you and check on me?"

"Parkie!" he exclaimed before I could answer.

"So, you win Game One and then play different guys the second game," he continued. "You should win anyway, but if not you get a split and everyone got a chance to start."

"That easy huh?"

"Yep, that easy," Michael answered.

"You know all those guys loved me," he smirked.

"Yes, I do" I chuckled.

"I sure wish you would be there," I sobbed.

"I will be," he winked.

And I was alone again on the bench.

CHAPTER 25

* * * * * *

Game Day — Angel in the Dugout

I managed to get dressed and pack everything I needed for my first game back. It took some deep breaths to push through, but it felt good to put my baseball gear back on and think about baseball.

First pitch was scheduled for 10:00 am. Our players were scheduled to arrive at 8:00 for batting practice on the field. I arrived at the school at 7:00. I had always prided myself on being on time, and I had always loved spending time in the stillness and quiet of the school and the baseball field before anyone else arrives.

But today, the stillness and quiet were not my friends.

The rising sun offered sufficient light as I opened the back door to the school and made my way to the equipment room. A shortcut through the main gymnasium is the quickest route to our baseball equipment, stored in a room just off the smaller, secondary gym.

I reached for the door but stopped, suddenly trembling.

Just beyond that door was the corner of the main gym; the same corner of the gym where our coaching staff always gathered before and after every practice; the same corner of the gym where Michael and I had our last conversation together.

God how I wished he could be waiting for me on the other side.

I was not ready to see or stand on that spot. I took my hand off the door and proceeded to take the long way around to another entrance to the equipment room, bypassing the main gym.

This was not going to be easy.

I performed the same routine I had done on several Saturday mornings the last four years. I walked through the quiet halls of the school and picked up the umpire checks from my mailbox in the school office. I drove from the school parking lot to the baseball field parking lot a block away. I unlocked the gate to Redbird field.

I opened up the press box. I sat in the quiet of the press box and looked out on the vast expanse of the bright green and brown playing field. I sat alone with my thoughts in the empty and eerily quiet stadium, and wrote out our game one lineup card.

I loved the stillness of being alone in a ballpark before all the players and parents descended on it for the day.

It was the same routine I had done many times before. But this time, it was distinctly different.

I got down to the dugout and arranged my equipment bag and briefcase in my usual spot at the end of the dugout. I got the box of brand new game balls out and unwrapped 12 of them. I pulled five index cards I would use during the game to track at-bats and take notes.

I sat on the top of the dugout bench and looked out at the sparkling green and brown field turf, starting to reflect the early morning sun. I looked up at the clear blue sky. I took one of the blank index cards and wrote a few notes to myself for reminders during the game.

- Glorify God
- Remember Michael
- Encourage them
- Love them
- Philippians 4:13

As I finished with my notes, I heard footsteps coming down the stairs. Of course the first player to arrive was Travis Auer, our senior leader.

"Good morning Coach," he said with a smile.

I wanted to return his greeting, but the words got stuck. I jumped up off the bench and gave him a hug. The hug lingered as we both thought about Michael and fought against tears.

The players arrived one by one, and one by one I gave each a hug. There was a minimum of chatter as they put on their game shoes and prepared for pregame batting practice. Once they were all ready, I called everyone over.

I stared up at the clear blue and cloudless sky, trying to gather myself as I tried to get the day off on the right start.

"Men – what a beautiful day for baseball. I am sure Michael has something to do with that. It's a great day to take batting practice. It's a great day to play two games. We are going to take batting practice and play two games on this glorious day that God has made, and we are going to have fun doing it – because that is exactly what Michael would want us to do."

"I am so glad to be back here with you guys. Michael loved being your coach and he loved each and every one of you. Every player is going to start at least one of the games today. There is absolutely no doubt in my mind Michael would want that today."

"Michael loved pre-game BP on a day like this. I want you to have fun during BP. I want you to have fun during the game – but I also want you to play hard. Support each other. Encourage each other. Play hard. Play to win. Have fun doing it. That is what Michael wants from us today. That is what Michael expects from us today"

I raised my hand signaling for everyone to huddle up. All hands were raised and touching as one team above our heads. "MC on three," I said. "One, two…

"MC!" they yelled in unison.

He had to have heard us.

Even the pregame meeting between the coaches and umpires had a strange and different feel. I knew the two umpires assigned to the game, but you could tell they were struggling to find the right words to say before covering the ground rules.

Josh Roop was the Tri-Valley head coach. I can't say I knew him well, but I had met him a few times at various Fellowship of Christian Athletes events, and I knew him as a man of strong faith. Knowing it was my first game back, Coach Roop asked me if we were doing anything special.

"Michael loved God and he loved playing second base," I said. "I would love to see any kids who want to, from both teams, meet at second base after the National Anthem for a prayer."

"Perfect – you got it," he responded.

More love, more Jesus.

After our meeting with the umpires was concluded both teams lined up on the field for the national anthem. As I've done thousands of time, I took my hat off and held it in my hand over my heart.

But this national anthem was far different.

I looked down, wanting to see Michael in that line. He wasn't there. My back was to the bleachers as the anthem blared so I knew the fans gathered couldn't see the tears streaming down my face, but I wondered if they could see my shoulders shuddering as I cried.

The Star Spangled Banner ended and the coaches stayed at home plate while the players from both teams jogged to second base for a prayer. It was such a beautiful site. Eighteen U-High players in their white uniforms trimmed in black, green and gold. Fifteen Tri-Valley players in their royal blue jerseys with gold trim. All players on one knee, holding hands, heads all bowed.

Coach Roop saw me struggling and lovingly placed his arm around me as I wept. We bowed our heads. No words were needed.

From that point on, we did everything we would normally do for a Saturday doubleheader. But there was nothing normal about the day.

The players jogged back to their respective dugouts, and I shook Coach Roop's hand and walked back to join our guys for our pre-game huddle.

As the game started, I began settling into my routine. Pacing in the dugout. Tracking outcomes on my note cards. Trying to think several at-bats ahead. In the back of my mind, I kept thinking about my commitment to have each player start a game. Key to that plan was a certain comfort level we would win the first game with our best players on the field.

And when we scored a run in each of the first two innings I was feeling pretty good about my decision.

Then Tri-Valley scored nine runs in the 4th inning.

The two conference games and the game with in-town rival Normal Community had left us pretty thin in terms of pitching options. We started 6'6 sophomore Austin Galindo, a hard throwing right-hander. Austin could throw it through a brick wall. The problem was, he sometimes had trouble hitting the wall.

After a couple good innings Austin got out of sync and walked the leadoff hitter. You could see Austin dial down the velocity to find the strike zone. The next hitter lined a single to right field.

In our pre-game meeting Coach Paxson, our pitching coach, and I discussed not letting Austin go too long and the primary goal being to help him gain some confidence. I decided to get him out now, hoping he could still feel good about himself.

That might have been a good decision, except the next pitcher in our plan for the day was Ryan Scott. Ryan is a great kid with a good arm, but he is an untested sophomore that has never really been a pitcher. He was learning on the job, and about to get a very hard lesson.

A couple hits, three walks, a hit-by-pitch, three wild pitches, and three errors that certainly didn't help any and we went from up 2-0 to down 9-2. Apparently I wasn't as concerned with Ryan's confidence, because I left him out there. At some point I suppose I was also thinking that the game is probably over and we can't burn any more pitchers.

I guess one good thing about giving up nine runs in an inning is that you have plenty of time to think about what you are going to say to your team when they come off the field.

Should I lay into them? Talk about all the walks? Tell them lack of focus caused errors and helped turn two or three runs into nine runs? I pulled the note cards from my back pocket. Glorify God. Honor Michael. Encourage them. Love them. Philippians 4:13.

I asked the team to gather in front of the dugout.

Eighteen sets of eyes were on me. You could see the shock and disappointment in their eyes. They were braced for a lashing.

I looked at them and smiled.

"How do you eat an elephant?" I started.

Puzzled doesn't even begin to describe the looks they gave me.

"One bite at a time gentlemen."

It didn't get much of a laugh, but there was a collective sigh and the mood lightened. Then I delivered a quick sermon that would become a consistent theme this season.

"We talk to you guys all the time about overcoming adversity. Is being down seven runs today adversity? Not compared to what you guys have already been through. You guys had to walk in to a room and tell your 22-year-old assistant coach goodbye. You had to attend his visitation and funeral. No high school baseball team should have to go through that. You guys have already handled more adversity than anyone can imagine. Down seven runs in a meaningless high school baseball game? That's nothing compared to what you've already been through. Don't think about seven runs. Think about scoring one. After we score one we'll think about getting another one. Just keep playing hard."

I put my hand up and they gathered around. One, two, three, "MC" we chanted.

We scored three runs in our half of the inning to make it 9-5.

We scored another run in the 5th to make it 9-6. Kendall Warner, a senior first baseman turned pitcher, somehow baffled Tri-Valley with his funky sidearm delivery and kept them from scoring in the 5th inning. Sophomore Jon Rink, another position player just learning to pitch, pitched a scoreless 6th.

We scored three runs in the bottom of the 6th inning to tie the game 9-9.

Rink worked around an error in the top of the 7th and we came into the dugout needing a run for a dramatic come-from-behind win.

Our parents in the bleachers were standing and cheering like I have never seen or heard before in a regular season high school baseball game.

They had been through this nightmare with me and with their kids. You could sense they knew there was more at stake than just a comeback win in this meaningless, non-conference, non-tournament, regular season game.

Rink got hit by a pitch to lead off the inning, followed by a walk. Zach Falasz dropped down a perfect sacrifice bunt to move the runners over with one out. Kyler Ummel was walked intentionally to load the bases.

Travis Auer came to the plate.

He was as close with Michael as anyone on the team.

The script was writing itself.

On a 1-1 count, Travis lined a sharp single and Rink scored! Everyone sprinted to Travis and mauled him like we had just won another state championship!

You just don't win games when you make five errors and give up nine runs in one inning.

With tears in my eyes, I pointed to the sky and thanked our angel.

CHAPTER 26

· · · · · · ·

Different Issues, Different Answers

We lost the second game of our doubleheader with Tri-Valley, but every player who didn't start in the first game was in the lineup for game two, and even a loss couldn't dampen the thrill of victory. Players went home happy. Parents went home happy. The day was over and a doubleheader split never felt so good.

Kelly, Jimmy, our nephew Jon, and several friends and family members were there when the game ended, a blessing that kept me from sitting in the dugout by myself to reflect on the day without my assistant coach and son.

I breathed a sigh of relief as the day ended. I had made it through the first of many "firsts."

We jumped right back into our game schedule the following Monday with a home game against intercity rival Bloomington. Our improved outlook took another hit with an ugly 14-9 loss to the hated crosstown Raiders.

The loss was even more depressing because of its implications for the post-season. Bloomington would be the host for our regional tournament, and this loss would likely mean being seeded behind them in the regional, and a tougher road to a coveted regional championship.

We were right back at it the next day with a conference road game at Prairie Central. The 22-9 win featured some fun for our players and every player on the roster got an at bat, but the win produced some alarming concerns for the coaching staff.

Of greatest concern was our best pitcher, junior Kyler Ummel, giving up nine runs to a bad team. The defense didn't help with several errors, and not all of them could be blamed on the bumpy infield.

The 22 runs were nice, especially when I heard a few of the players quoting Michael. "Never get tired of scoring runs," he would tell them. But we were also smart enough to realize those runs came at the expense of some awful pitching, the likes of which we would never see in the games that really mattered.

But a win is a win and always better than a loss. The best part of our evening was the postgame stop. A trip to Fairbury meant a Dairy Queen stop after the game for a meal plus ice cream on the way home, and both always tasted better after a win.

Having been an assistant coach for three years at U-High, I was well aware the tradition for road games was to have parents arrange sandwiches for the team to eat on the bus ride home.

It was one of the first things I changed when I was named head coach.

Because we shared our home field with Illinois State University baseball, we generally had more road dates on our schedule than home games. I couldn't stand the thought of cold sandwiches after all road games, so when I was asked about parent sandwich assignments at an initial parent meeting my first year on the job, our new plans of stopping for fast food after road games was announced.

I was amazed, and to be honest concerned, about the reaction from some parents. In my mind it was a win-win. They didn't have to hassle with arranging for sandwiches, and we got some variety and a warm dinner, even if it was fast food. You would have thought I had just outlawed the school mascot!

I think a small group of parents viewed this as the new coach exerting unreasonable control.

I just wanted an occasional Big Mac instead of a cold ham sandwich.

Well, that and in my experience postgame stops offered a nice chance for the team and coaching staff to unwind, bond, and build relationships. I stuck to my guns. It was fun after a win, and helped ease the pain after a loss. The players enjoyed the postgame stops, as I knew they would. It created memories and helped our team bond.

For this current group of kids, during this ridiculously unusual season, it provided additional welcome relief from horrible circumstances and constant reminders.

So we found ourselves at the Fairbury Dairy Queen.

I faced another first.

It was our first postgame stop without Michael.

I got such a kick out of our postgame meal stops when he was an assistant coach last spring. He would sit with the coaches and interact so professionally as we discussed various players and plays from the game just completed, and then would just as easily get up and visit a players table and interact with them. He would joke and laugh with the players, somehow juggling his role as coach, mentor, peer and friend. He had such an uncanny way with them.

Our normal practice at restaurants was for coaches to always order before players. Michael would probably be disappointed, but I opened the door for the players and told them to order first, while I fought back tears and thought about something else I would never get to do again.

I pulled a "Pay It Forward" card we had made with Michael's picture on it and gave the card and a $20 bill to Travis Auer. I told him to figure out a way to pay it forward. All the players started giving him money to add to the $20. The cashier looked on the verge of tears as she took the card and the money so the next $80 worth of orders would be paid.

I couldn't help but think "this one is for you, Michael" as I ordered my double cheeseburger and fries.

Wednesday marked the first day back since I returned with no game on the schedule. We needed to practice, and I was looking forward to a day off from making lineup decisions and worrying about a win or a loss.

It rained all day Wednesday so unfortunately our practice would have to be indoors. I had compiled a long list of errors, missed signs, and other mistakes we had made in our last four games. I was reviewing this long list of things to work on as I arrived at the gym. I reached for the gym door and remembered that was the corner I had avoided last Saturday. I took the long way around again so I could enter at the other end of the gym.

Before I could even find a new spot to put my jacket and briefcase, Kendall Warner hurried toward me across the gym floor.

"Coach you need to go see McLean," he said, short of breath. "He's in the equipment room crying."

The list of mistakes and corrections would have to wait.

McLean Conklin was a senior. He had entered the baseball program as a freshman, my first year as the head coach. I remember seeing him the first day of tryouts, a scrawny kid with limited skills. On that day four years ago I would have bet a lot of money that he would never contribute at the varsity level.

I would have lost a lot of money.

For the next four years, McLean worked as hard, if not harder, than any player in our program. He saw his future as a pitcher, and he spent off-seasons working with a private instructor to improve his velocity. He also threw himself into an off-season strength and conditioning program.

By the time his junior season rolled around he was bigger, faster, stronger and threw harder than I ever could have imagined possible out of that small, skinny kid that showed up as a freshman.

Unfortunately, all that work came at a price. He was unable to pitch or play the outfield his junior season because of a recurring issue with his elbow.

The summer after his junior season, a doctor decided it was some kind of nerve issue in his elbow, and McLean had surgery.

When our spring season started McLean was on a rehab program the doctor prescribed for him to be able to pitch again.

He wasn't pitching, but he was doing a great job in the outfield for us and was one of our most consistent hitters. He was hitting in the middle of the order and driving in big runs.

And now, he was apparently in the equipment room crying.

As I crossed the gym floor I was certain Kendall was exaggerating when he used the term "crying."

He wasn't.

I walked in the room and McLean looked up from having his head cradled in his arm. Tears streamed down his cheeks. His shoulders heaved up and down. He was making the same "can't catch my breath" wails a child makes during a tantrum.

I closed the door.

I didn't ask what was wrong and I didn't give him a chance to tell me; I just went over and wrapped my arms around him like a father would hold his distraught son.

He put his head on my shoulder and continued to weep as he slowly gained control.

After a long embrace, the sobs subsided and McLean lifted his head off my shoulder and stepped back, ready to tell me what was wrong.

"I got called in to Mr. Evans' office," he said. Mr. Evans is the assistant principal. "He told me I am failing two classes and not eligible to play."

"He says there is nothing I can do. I can't play tomorrow and I have to miss all the games this weekend."

The sobbing and heavy breathing started again.

Ordinarily, when a player is not eligible for academic reasons, I've shown very little sympathy and figure they are getting what they deserve for not trying hard enough in the classroom.

But something was out of whack. McLean had always been a good student. In three years, I don't ever recall his name showing up on the weekly eligibility list, which means he's never been getting worse than a "C" in any class.

"Are you failing the classes?" I asked.

"Yes," he replied. "I have some assignments I didn't get turned in."

"Why didn't you get them turned in?"

His shoulders started shaking again. He dropped his head to try and hide the tears. He sobbed, but didn't reply.

There was something more going on here than missed assignments.

"Is it Michael?" I asked.

The tears came hard and he turned away, burying his head in his arm resting on a cabinet as he cried.

I stepped toward him and put my arm around him.

"McLean," I said. "I know it's hard, but we are going to get through this. I promise we can get through this. But for me to help you get through this you have to be honest and tell me what is going on."

More time passed and the sobbing slowed again. He lifted his head. I backed away.

"Talk to me McLean. We've been together for three years. What's going on?"

"I can't concentrate coach," he said. "I can't focus. I can't stop thinking about Michael. I close my eyes and see him lying in the casket."

My first thought was that I'm not a grief counselor, and he may need some professional help.

I also figured nobody knew more about what he was feeling than I did.

I also knew I was about to cross a line the school administrators would tell me not to cross.

"McLean, do you believe in God?"

"Yes," he answered, though somewhat hesitantly, clearly caught off-guard by the question.

"I don't understand why this happened to Michael," I said. "But to believe in God means we have faith; faith that His ways are higher than our ways; faith that He has a plan for Michael and a plan for us and His plan is perfect; faith that Michael is alive and happy in Heaven."

"Do you have that faith, Mclean?"

He looked up. The tears had stopped.

"Yes," he answered, with less hesitation.

"Michael isn't gone McLean, he's just in a different place and we will see him again."

"I don't understand everything either and I miss him too," I added. "This faith is what I hang onto. This hope is what keeps me going."

He nodded his head.

"Ok, tell me about these assignments you didn't get turned in."

He described in detail various past due assignments in two different classes. He told me who the teachers were and described his conversation with Mr. Evans.

I quickly formulated a plan.

"We are going to get through this together ok?"

He again nodded his head.

"I'm not sure there is anything we can do about the game tomorrow and I can't promise anything, but if you can get these assignments turned in I will do my best to convince the teachers, and Mr. Evans, to let you play this weekend."

McLean stopped me. "Mr. Evans told me nothing could be done before Monday."

"Like I said, I can't promise anything, but you let me worry about Mr. Evans. He knows we've been through a lot. I think I can convince him, but you've got to get the work turned in."

"I want you to leave now. You are excused from practice. I want you to go home, tell your mom and dad about what happened and about this conversation. Tell them everything. You get these assignments done and submitted, and let me see if I can get something done before the weekend."

He smiled. We hugged and he headed out the door.

He wasn't in uniform the next night, but did get his past due assignments turned in during the day.

I sent an email to Mr. Evans and copied the Athletic Director and Principal, reminding them McLean had never been a problem, and reminding them how much our team is still grieving. They all replied like I knew they would. The teachers graded the assignments quickly, the standard eligibility timing was waived, and McLean was able to play on the weekend.

Michael's words echoed in my head. "More love, more Jesus."

CHAPTER 27

• • • • • • • •

He Reminds Me of a Young Michael Collins

The season proceeded as could be expected from a team with its two best pitchers unable to pitch, loaded with sophomores and juniors, and living through a tumultuous and unthinkable tragedy.

There were certainly some additional high points.

We took our annual planned overnight trip to the Pleasant Plains Invitational tournament. We made the trip even more memorable with an exciting 3-0 weekend with three close and thrilling wins, albeit against smaller school opponents.

But we certainly had our fair share of additional disappointments on the field as well.

We had some nice conference wins, countered by some difficult conference losses.

Many of our struggles could be pinned on our defense, and on any high school baseball team the shortstop is the key spot and anchor of the infield. Our shortstop was junior Nick "Trickster" Mosele, and his up and down season on defense thus far mirrored our up and down season as a team.

We came to practice on a Friday afternoon after back-to-back beatings, an unthinkable 12-1 loss to archrival Central Catholic, and a 12-2 thumping by eventual conference champion Mahomet.

Consecutive run-rule losses left the coaching staff in a sour mood, and as we gathered just outside the end of the dugout prior to practice our focus was on Nick and the ever-critical shortstop position.

"Our pitching hasn't been great, but our defense isn't helping," Coach Paxson stated. "What do you think about trying somebody else at shortstop."

Before I could respond, Coach Haws jumped in. "I agree," he proclaimed confidently. "I think we need to move Rink over to short. I thought he was our best shortstop before the season started and I still do," he added.

His reference took my mind back to the pre-season, back to that corner of the gym I now did everything to avoid, and a conversation the coaching staff had about who would be our shortstop.

We were considering several options. Senior Tyler May had played shortstop his junior year, but not very well. I loved Tyler and he would no doubt have a place on the field, but to be as successful as possible I thought we needed a change.

Jon Rink was another option, but he was an untested sophomore.

We stood in the corner and watched all of them taking ground balls off the wood floor.

"He's our starting shortstop," I heard Michael say as we watched junior Nick Mosele field a ground ball off the gym floor at an early March practice.

The confidence and emphasis in his voice made it clear there was really no need, in his mind, for further discussion.

Michael always had a soft spot in his heart and a tremendous amount of belief in Nick. His mentorship of Nick started a year ago, when Nick was trying to earn a varsity spot as a 5'6, 130 pound sophomore.

A varsity spot certainly wasn't a given as a sophomore. He had great baseball actions but was, at best, undersized and looked like he might snap in half if he tried a bench press with any weight on the bar. To make matters worse, he told us before tryouts that he couldn't throw because of a sore elbow. Small and can't throw – not exactly a recipe for making a varsity squad as a sophomore.

The first night of tryouts that year Michael strolls up to me and says "that kid has to make the team?"

"Michael, he's small and has a bad elbow," I replied. "Why in the world would he make our varsity team."

Michael explained. "Since he couldn't throw, he came over and asked me what he should do while the rest of the team was throwing. I told him to drop down and give me 25 pushups – and he immediately dropped down to do it!"

Michael laughed as he told the story. "I'm a college kid who is helping out. Any kid who will do that, as soon as I say it, with no questions asked, needs to make the team."

Michael gave me that mischievous smile – the one that says you may think I am crazy, but I am dead serious. "Besides, he reminds me of a young Michael Collins," he said.

Nick made the team as a sophomore. He played sparingly, but fit in great and worked hard. He played every game on our school team the following summer, and got better and better as the summer progressed.

And here we are, 25 games into the season, talking about the shortstop position yet again.

I was baffled by some of Nick's ups and downs on defense. "Shortstop is a tough place to play and I knew it would take awhile for him to settle in, but I thought he would be better than this by now,"

"Maybe we aren't getting enough reps," I added. "He used to take extra ground balls after every practice. I never see him taking extra ground balls anymore," I lamented.

Travis Auer was standing a few feet from the coaches as we continued watching Nick and the infielders take ground balls.

He waited until there was a pause in our discussion.

"Hey coach, can I talk to you for a minute," he asked.

I led him down the right field line past the dugout and away from any coaches and players.

"What's up Travis?" I started.

"You know why Nick isn't taking ground balls after practice don't you?' he asked.

I didn't know if the question was rhetorical, but I'm sure he could tell from my puzzled look I didn't have the answer.

"Michael was the one who always hit ground balls to him after practice," he shared, his voice starting to quiver. It seemed like he wanted to add something, but he stopped for fear of breaking down.

I sat for a minute, somewhat stunned by the revelation. I didn't know whether to be mad at myself for not being aware enough to notice, or at Travis for not saying something earlier.

So I blurted the first thing that came to mind.

"Why didn't somebody else hit him ground balls," I asked.

"We've tried. He told us he doesn't want anyone hitting him ground balls but Michael."

I gave Travis a hug, told him thanks for letting me know, and we went back to re-join practice.

When practice ended, I told Nick I had a couple questions for him.

I asked if he had to leave right away, or could he stay and talk for a few minutes. He said he could stay.

I told him I had to run up to the press box, but I would be back in a minute. I wanted to allow time for the rest of the team to leave.

Nick was alone in the dugout when I returned, sitting on the bench next to his bag, packed and ready to go.

I sat down next to him.

"What's up coach?"

"Nick, how come you don't take extra ground balls after practice anymore?"

He paused. It was clearly not the question or topic he expected.

After a very brief moment, his chin dropped to his chest, his shoulders began to shake, and he started crying uncontrollably.

I scooted closer and put my arm around him. He immediately reached to get his arms around me and bury his head into my chest. The tears flowed for seconds that seemed like minutes. His sobs seemed to echo in the empty dugout.

Nick loosened his grasp and pulled back. He looked at me as if wanting to speak, but not knowing what to say. So I spoke.

"Michael loved you Nick, and he loved staying after practice and hitting you ground balls."

He was looking downward but nodded.

"I would give anything in the world to be able to bring Michael back so he could hit you ground balls Nick, and I know you would too. But I can't."

Still sobbing, his eyes stayed on the floor but he nodded again.

"Look at me Nick," I asked.

He looked up. Tear marks stained his face. It killed me to see this innocent young man in such an exciting time of life fractured and scarred by this unthinkable tragedy, desperately missing his mentor and friend.

"Do you believe in Heaven Nick," I asked. I felt comfortable broaching this subject with Nick because I knew the answer.

"Yes," he muttered softly.

"Do you believe Michael is in Heaven?"

He nodded yes.

"I do too Nick. There is no doubt in my mind, and I believe he is closer to us than we might think."

"I miss him Nick. I know you do too."

"I can't bring Michael back but I'll tell you what I can do. I can hit you ground balls, and we can believe there is a good chance Michael is watching both of us."

"Can we do that Nick?"

"OK," he said. He unzipped his bag and pulled out his glove. He got up, wiped away the remaining tears, and jogged out to his spot at shortstop. I wiped tears from my eyes as I grabbed a bucket of baseballs and a fungo bat.

For the next 20 minutes, neither of us spoke a word. The only sound heard was the thwack of a ball against a bat and Nick dropping the balls he fielded into a bucket.

I hit ground balls right at him. I hit ground balls to his left. I hit ground balls to his right. I hit slow rollers in front of him.

When my large bucket of baseballs was empty, I waived Nick in. He gathered up a few loose balls, put them in his bucket, and walked in carrying his now overflowing bucket of baseballs.

He was out of breath from the non-stop barrage. His gray shirt was covered in perspiration. I put my arm around him and walked alongside him toward the dugout.

"How did that feel," I asked.

"Good," he responded.

"You looked good," I said. "Let's get out of here."

Nick packed up his bag. I gathered up my papers and went to lock up the equipment room at the end of the dugout. When I walked back, Nick was at the top of the steps waiting for me to leave.

I decided to take a rather unusual and perhaps risky step.

"Nick, at our very first practice this spring, Michael told me you should be our shortstop. He believed in you, and so do I. I know you loved Michael and I know you have a lot to deal with. One thing you don't have to worry about is whether or not you will play. Michael was right – you ARE our shortstop. And I don't care what happens from here on out – good days and bad days – you will be our shortstop."

"Thanks coach," Nick said.

He opened the dugout gate leading up to the concourse overlooking the field. I followed him up the steps, and he seemed to have an extra bounce I hadn't seen for awhile. We walked together toward the entrance gate at the front of the stadium.

He kept walking towards his car and I stopped so that I could get the press box and front gate locked up.

"Hey Nick," I called.

He stopped and turned.

"I love you."

He smiled.

"I love you too coach."

As I worked to get the front gate locked I heard a loud clang. It came from our home team dugout Nick and I had just left. I was certain the stadium was empty, but it sure sounded like the dugout gate had just closed.

I paused.

Maybe it was the wind.

Maybe it was…

I smiled.

CHAPTER 28

● ● ● ● ● ● ●

Field of Dreams

As we entered the home stretch of the season, we were 16-9. Any hope of achieving our annual goal of a conference championship was gone.

We started down this home stretch with a game I was so thrilled about when we were able to schedule it last December. The opponent would be Chillicothe IVC, but it wasn't the opposition that was so intriguing for me, it was the location.

We would be playing at Dozer Field in Peoria, formerly known as O'Brien Field, the same field where we won the state championship two years before.

It was my second year as head coach, only the third baseball state championship in the history of the school, and a crowning achievement for any high school coach in the state of Illinois.

How important was the state championship to me?

I recalled the conversation I had last winter on a shopping trip to Peoria with Kelly and two family members. As we crossed the Illinois river and neared the Peoria city limits, you could see the lights of the baseball stadium rising above the downtown district.

"There's O'Brien Field," I stated, pointing toward the lights. "The site of the greatest moment of my life."

After a brief but awkward silence Kelly asked "where does the day we got married and the birth of your two sons rank?"

"OK," I chuckled. "The fourth greatest moment in my life."

Two years removed from that state championship, we took the forty-five minute bus ride from Normal to Peoria. Only five people on the bus were part of that state championship team.

As the bus motored toward Peoria there was some idle chatter, but it was mostly quiet as the players got lost in whatever music they had blaring through their headphones.

I sat in the relative quiet and thought about some of the memories from that unforgettable weekend in 2012. I was certain they would come flooding back to me when we pulled up to the field and entered the stadium

I was sure I would remember the spot between home plate and first base where I got the most glorious, wet and sticky Gatorade bath.

I was certain I would go back to the end of the first base dugout, remembering the pure joy as our team piled on top of each other after the final out was recorded.

I thought I would remember the seat just outside the dugout where Kelly stood and gave me a good luck kiss before the game, and a celebratory hug after the game as I cried tears of happiness and relief.

I should have known better.

As the players changed shoes and prepared in the spacious first base dugout, the same dugout we occupied in the state championship game, I took a walk towards right field on the plush green grass of this miniature version of a major league ballpark.

I walked on the vibrant and perfectly manicured grass and scanned the empty grandstands surrounding this field where so many dreams had come true two years ago.

But the flood of 2012 championship memories didn't happen. As I took in the scents and scenery of this baseball treasure, the memories from 2012 rushing to my mind were now linked and haunted by the pain and loss of two months ago.

I stared at the seat next to the dugout and remembered Kelly telling me about the days she had just spent in Enid, Oklahoma watching Michael at the Junior College World Series, and the good wishes he had told her to give me since he couldn't be at my game.

I saw the spot of my 2012 Gatorade bath, but instead of the state championship trophy presentation, I recalled getting home after the game and choosing to miss a postgame party so I could go and share the trophy and moment with Michael, and hear about his final bus ride home as a Heartland Hawk.

I looked toward the concourse and remembered being up there by myself after the game in 2012 with the state championship trophy, but I recalled the tears of joy and relief being mixed with tears of sadness and regret because Michael hadn't been there to share it with me.

This is not how I wanted this special game, at this special place, to go. Thankfully, I was now deep enough in right field so the players in the dugout weren't able to see me crying as I thought about all the life here on earth I would not be able to experience with Michael.

I walked toward the right field line, to the same spot where our team had prayed before the game in 2012, and the same spot this team would pray on in about an hour.

I got on one knee and bowed my head.

"Father God. Thank You for the 22 years you gave me with Michael. Please give me strength to get through this game. Holy Spirit please fill me. Give me the right words to help this group of kids enjoy this night and create good memories on this special field. Amen."

I stood, looked to the sky and whispered, "tonight would be a good night for you to be with us Michael."

We won 1-0.

It wasn't a state championship, but it had that kind of exciting feel to it. It was a close game against a storied Chillicothe program with several recent state championship appearances and titles.

It was a perfect night for baseball in a ballpark with a big-league feel, and our guys came through with our most exciting win of the season.

Zach Frey singled and scored in the 5th inning, and it would be the only run we needed.

Twenty-five games into the season and we had not recorded a shutout. We had a no-hitter earlier, but even managed to give up a run in that game.

Junior Kyler Ummel was crafty and dominant on the mound, hurling the complete game win with less than 100 pitches.

Our defense was brilliant.

And most importantly, shortstop Nick Mosele was flawless.

He made plays to his right, plays to his left, and all the routine plays at him. He artfully turned two huge double plays in critical spots to squash a pair of rallies.

He played with a level of effort and grace that sparked everyone around him to play better and with more confidence.

He played like a weight had somehow been lifted off his back.

He reminded me of a young Michael Collins.

Another piece of the puzzle was falling into place.

CHAPTER 29

● ● ● ● ● ● ●

Senior Night

Kelly has taken thousands of wonderful photographs of Jimmy and Michael during their days of travel and high school baseball. Only a few from those thousands have been enlarged to 8 X 10, elevated to framed status, and chosen to adorn our basement walls.

Two of the lucky few framed memories hanging on the walls in perpetuity are from their respective "senior nights" at University High School and Normal West.

I had tried very hard to make senior night special for our baseball program in my first three years as head coach.

This one needed to be even more special.

Coaches in all high school sports are often conflicted around playing time and lineup decisions on these nights designated to honor senior players. Coaches wrestle between the pull of honoring seniors by playing some who would not ordinarily play, and the pressure of playing to win. I have struggled myself with these decisions.

I recalled my visit from Michael on the bench at the Ironwood Golf Course the Saturday morning I returned to coaching.

On this senior night, I would not struggle with the decision.

Two nights before our "senior night" game with Rantoul, the coaching staff gathered at the end of dugout. Normally, I ask Coach Paxson for his thoughts on the starter and relief pitching assignments for each game. This time I didn't ask.

"I plan on Tyler Gilliam being the starting pitcher," I stated.

His puzzled look clearly indicated that was not the direction he was thinking.

"Zach Frey is ready," he responded. Zach was a hard-throwing sophomore who had become one of our best pitchers.

"It's senior night," I countered. "All of the seniors are going to start, and I want Tyler on the mound."

Coach Paxson had been a head coach for 10 years prior to joining my staff as an assistant. I had a great deal of respect for his background and success as a head coach.

"How did you handle senior night at Brimfield coach?" I asked.

"We always had some type of ceremony to honor our seniors," he answered. "But we played to win."

I thought about his response.

"We are playing to win too. But we are going to do it with all our seniors on the field. They deserve that opportunity."

Admittedly, the decision was easier given we had already been eliminated from the conference race.

"What if we had a chance to win the conference?" Coach Paxson asked.

"That's easy," I smiled. "We would make a different game our senior night."

It felt good to be able to laugh together.

On previous senior nights we have introduced each senior and his parents before the game, and I say a few words about each player. Two of the junior moms were helping to organize the evening festivities, and

I told them I wasn't sure I could talk about these guys without crying, and hated to start the night that way. They convinced me I didn't need to speak before the game.

What a great decision that turned out to be.

The seniors were introduced one by one, and they escorted their parents onto the field. I cried as I watched these seniors and these parents and thought about everything we had been through together, especially in the last two months. After they were all lined up, I walked out and hugged each player, each mom, and each dad.

Tears flowed as with each hug I thanked them for all their support.

Speaking at that point would have been an impossible task.

All seven seniors took the field, including Travis Auer. Travis hadn't played since doctors found a broken bone in his elbow. He was still unable to swing a bat or throw a baseball. So we put him at third base and told Tyler the first pitch of the game had to be a ball, and then removed Travis from the game after the first pitch.

The smile lighting up Travis' face as he trotted off the field to warm applause from the crowd told us how much he appreciated the gesture.

Rantoul started their ace on the mound, a hard throwing Division I prospect, and jumped on us with two runs in the first inning.

It said a lot about this group of seniors when we responded by scoring three runs in the bottom of the first.

We lost on senior night 7-3.

We gathered on the concourse over-looking the bright turf diamond. A few younger brothers of current players were still running around on the field. I stood in front of the players, their parents, grandparents, family members, and friends.

I looked up to speak. The people looking at me had become more like family than any team of athletes and parents I had ever been associated with.

I wanted to speak, but felt a wave of tears starting to arrive instead. I looked down, pausing to gather myself. My voice waivered, but I got started.

"These seven seniors will always have a very special place in my heart. I expect a lot from seniors, and they have all been amazing leaders and teammates under the most unimaginable circumstances. I would like to introduce each one of them individually."

I asked Parker Schaab to join me. I put my arm around him.

I knew what I wanted to share about Parker, but I also knew it wouldn't be easy getting through it. My voice quivered as I started.

"Every team should have a Parker Schaab on it. Parker has been on the varsity team for two years. He didn't get a lot of at-bats, but he showed up at every game and every practice for two years and worked hard. No matter what we've asked him to do he has given his best effort. He has never complained, never been late, and never been a problem. This year, when I've been gone and we've been short of coaches, he has stepped in to throw batting practice so guys could get some extra swings. We are a better team because Parker is a part of it. I am a better person for having known Parker.

I will never forget walking into the waiting room at the hospital after they took Michael back for his first surgery that Saturday morning. Parker was the first person I saw."

My voice trailed off. I turned and gave Parker a hug.

"I love you Parker."

"I love you too, Coach."

I asked Brendan Bond to join me in front of the crowd. I placed my arm around his shoulder.

"I am so proud of Brendan. I'm sure I haven't told him that nearly enough the last two years. Brendan may have improved more in the last two years than anybody on the team. He showed that tonight with three hits against a very good team! I'm sure he wasn't in the lineup as much as he would have wanted, and that's a good thing. I want everyone in this program to have the desire to play more. Whether Brendan was in the lineup or not this year, he has been a great teammate, and that is the best compliment I can give a player. I am so proud of him for having a special senior night!"

I gave Brendan a hug.

"I love you Brendan."

"I love you too, Coach."

I then called up Tyler Gilliam and put my arm around him.

"Tyler is another great example of how much hard work pays off. He didn't pitch much for us as a junior. Last summer on our school team we told him he would get plenty of work, and we told him we were going to take him outside his comfort zone. We know Tyler isn't going to throw his fastball by hitters, so in the summer we made him pitch differently. We made him throw first pitch curveballs and off-speed pitches when he was behind in counts rather than fastballs. They call it pitching backward, and it probably meant giving up some hits or walking guys in the summer he could have gotten out with fastballs. But Tyler bought into the plan. He worked hard last summer and he got better. That hard work has paid off this spring with some good outings on the mound and a couple key wins. He's been a great student and a great example for his teammates. Thank you Tyler!"

I hugged Tyler.

"I love you Tyler."

"I love you too, Coach."

I asked Kendall Warner to join me in front of the players and parents.

"I love what Kendall has done this year. We always talk about baseball being a game of failure. We talk about perseverance and mental toughness and extra effort and never giving up. Kendall modeled all of those for us this season. He was our starting first baseman to start the season, but he struggled. He found himself sitting on the bench a few games. But he didn't sulk. He didn't pout. He supported whoever played first base that day. He worked hard in practice every day to get better. He even pitched when we needed him to pitch. And now he is back at first base giving us great at bats and ready to have a great post-season."

I turned and hugged Kendall.

"I love you Kendall."

"Thanks for sticking by me Coach. I love you too."

I asked for McLean Conklin to join me.

"When McLean walked into the gym for tryouts as a freshman, he was so small and skinny I almost cut him right on the spot. McLean has worked harder to make himself a better baseball player than anyone I know. He has worked hard in the weight room to get stronger and faster. He has worked hard in the batting cage to be a better hitter. He has worked hard on his throwing mechanics to improve his arm strength. He is a poster child for what happens when you have a dream and are willing to sacrifice to make that dream come true. He has been a huge part of our success the last two years. I am so proud of what he has accomplished, and so thankful I didn't cut him."

I hugged McLean tightly.

"I love you McLean."

"Thanks for everything Coach. I love you too."

I called Tyler May up and he stood next to me.

"One of the best compliments a coach can give a player is to call him selfless, and Tyler was as selfless this year as I've ever seen a player be in all my years of coaching.

Tyler was the starting second baseman as a sophomore on our state championship team. He was our starting shortstop last year. This year, before the season even started, we asked him to move to third base. He said, "sure Coach." Then a few games into the season we asked him to move to the outfield. He had never really played outfield, but he said "whatever the team needs Coach." He has been great in the outfield and has been our most consistent hitter. He has probably been our most valuable player to this point, and I truly believe his willingness to do what is best for the team has been a huge part of his success. He has played the game the way it is supposed to be played every day as part of this team, and I love him for what he has meant to U-High baseball."

I hugged Tyler.

"I love you Tyler."

"Thanks for a great four years Coach. I love you too."

I introduced Travis Auer.

"I don't know where to start with Travis. He has faced one setback after another the last several months. He was our best pitcher as a junior, but he knew he wouldn't be able to pitch his senior season after having Tommy John surgery. So he grabbed a bat, told me the doctor said he could play first base or DH, and became a huge part of our offense early in the spring. Then they found a broken bone in his elbow they somehow didn't see during the surgery, and he was told he couldn't play at all the rest of the season. Throw in what happened to Michael, and I think a lot of guys might have walked away at that point. Travis didn't walk away. He has been at every practice. He has been at every game. He has been willing to do whatever he can possibly do to help the team in any way he can. It's that kind of attitude that will make Travis successful no matter what he does in life."

I grabbed Travis in a big hug.

"I love you Travis. Michael would be very proud of you."

"Thank you Coach. I love you too Coach." I could feel him shake as he cried in my arms.

The seven seniors stood in a line together. As was our tradition, seven teammates came forward and presented them with a bag of gifts. This year the bag included a picture of the seven seniors together and a memory book with various pictures from the season.

The seniors stayed in a line as I offered some closing remarks.

"These seven guys are the first group of seniors I've had since they were freshmen. They know I demand a lot from players in our program. They know we've always tried to set high expectations. And they know I expect a lot out of seniors.

The question for every senior class should be – is the program better than when we got here as freshmen. There is no doubt this class can answer "yes" to that question!

This team has been through something this year that no high school baseball team should ever have to go through. This group of seniors has provided unbelievable leadership in helping us get through it, and I love all of them for it."

As I thought about my final words, I could sense tears starting to swell. I paused. As I looked at these seven seniors and the family of teammates and parents looking at them, I wasn't sure I could get my final words out. My voice quaked.

"I know this. Michael would be very proud of all of you."

The parents and family members could tell by my quivering voice I was done, and they began to applaud loudly. Each senior came to me one by one for another hug, and then joined the crowd of teammates, family and friends.

I have been part of hundreds of meetings involving players and parents during my coaching career. The spirit of "family" present on that concourse was like nothing I had ever experienced before.

The love on that concourse was palpable.

I closed my eyes and could see Michael smiling.

This turbulent season had certainly been a long, emotional, and exhausting ride for these seven seniors, their teammates, and their parents.

We were all hoping the best was still ahead of us.

PART IV

Spirit Rising

"I can do everything through Christ,
who gives me strength."
Philippians 4:13

CHAPTER 30

• • • • • • •

We Believe

After practice the following week, the players had changed their shoes, packed their gear in their bags, and now gathered near the on-deck circle just outside our home dugout, waiting for my closing comments and to be dismissed.

I told them I had a surprise for them, and they watched as I hurried up the steps to the press box.

I sat in the press box overlooking the beautiful, sun-drenched stadium and looked out at this group of players and coaches. We had been through so much together the last couple of months. Several of them were looking up at the press box, trying to figure out what they might be getting as a surprise.

I opened up the box of shirts I had ordered for the players and looked at one. It was a bright gold shirt. Emblazoned on the front was the "MCstrong" logo we had created in Michael's honor, with the cross, in place of the "t" so prominent.

Tears started to fill my eyes.

I flipped the shirt over.

The back simply read "We Believe."

I had heard the song on the radio a couple weeks earlier and immediately knew it was meant for us. I turned the speaker system almost as high as it would go, pushed play, and heard the Newsboys song start to fill the stadium.

> In this time of desperation
> When all we know is doubt and fear
> There is only One Foundation
> We believe, We believe

Eyes still moist, I grabbed the box and headed back down to the field.

As I started down the steps, the applause started.

Each and every player was clapping.

The clapping got louder and louder as I made my way down the steps and neared the field. They all had huge smiles on their faces. I smiled through my tears. The music seemed to get louder as the chorus played.

> We believe in God the Father
> We believe in Jesus Christ
> We believe in the Holy Spirit
> And He's given us new life

I dropped the box on the turf and stood facing the players. I held up one shirt, showing them the front with the logo.

"I hope the first thing you see when you look at this logo is the cross," I said. "We created this logo for the Michael Collins Foundation, but Michael would tell you the focus should always be on Jesus."

I flipped the shirt around.

"I heard this song by the Newsboys last week and I just knew it was written for us," I told them. "Most importantly, I hope we believe together in God, and Michael is in Heaven, and we are all part of God's plan."

"But the shirt has two meanings," I added.

"I don't know if anyone else believes we can win a regional championship, but I do, and I know you guys do too! It doesn't matter what anybody else thinks. The only thing that matters is you guys have to believe!"

As if on cue, the players began hooting and hollering and surrounded me with hands held high in the air.

Somebody yelled "Let's win this for MC."

"MC on three," somebody else screamed.

"One, two, three – MC!"

We were ready.

We believed!

CHAPTER 31

● ● ● ● ● ● ●

Dugout Visitor

After all the players and coaches had left, I went down to our dugout to get my laptop bag. I decided to spend a few minutes in the dugout by myself. I looked out over the now empty field, a mix of sun and shadows as the sun set and darkness neared.

For me, there is nothing quite like the still beauty of an empty ballpark to clear my mind. I closed my eyes and listened to the silence. My mind was far from clear.

Every postseason game is "Game Seven" in Illinois high school baseball. The state tournament series culminating in a single state champion in four different classes, 1A through 4A, is a single elimination tournament.

Win and advance. Lose and go home. Do or die.

I have been involved in high school baseball for 20 years and only once have I been part of a team that won its last game of the season and hoisted a state champion trophy.

And that was one more than most high school coaches ever know.

In every year but that one, I have been part of postgame huddles where seniors knew they had just played their last game.

Baseball in Illinois is a spring season, so school has often already ended. The incredible bonds that had been forged by these young men after years of going to school and playing baseball together were now broken with a loss. Tears always flowed during these postgame moments and the heartbreak over something they all loved coming to an end.

The bonds this group had formed because of what we had endured together were like nothing I had ever seen before.

A few weeks back they all wanted our nightmare to end, but now they were desperate for the season to continue.

I was torn.

Part of me wanted the season to end. The pain of doing this every day without Michael by my side, was at times unbearable.

Part of me wanted the season to never end, because that might make this nightmare all too real again.

Time alone in the dugout is meant to clear my head, not raise my anxiety level. I took a deep breath, closed my eyes and tried to relax. I felt a gentle breeze blow across the field and through the dugout.

Then the gate to the dugout opened.

Michael sat down on the bench next to me. As always, impeccably dressed in his baseball gear. His pants were the perfect length, showing just enough of his shoe; batting practice jacket fit just right to show off his narrow waist; hat on straight, with white Oakley sunglasses stylishly perched on top of his cap.

"Well, are they ready Big Hoss?" he asked, chuckling at the use of the nickname he knew wasn't my favorite.

"I don't know," I replied. "How much can you help us if we need it," I grinned.

"Not as much as you would like," he smirked.

God I missed that smile.

"I'd feel a lot better if you were coaching first base," I said.

"Me too," he agreed. "I was a great first base coach! Maybe the best first base coach ever!

"I don't know about that," I answered. "Your first base coach at Normal West was pretty good."

"Yeah, you weren't too bad," he smiled.

"I gotta go Dad," he said. "But go win a regional and quit worrying about me."

I heard the clink of the dugout gate and looked up.

I was alone in the dugout again.

CHAPTER 32

• • • • • • • •

It's Just Game Number 35

Crosstown rival Bloomington High School was playing host to our Illinois High School Association Class 3A Regional tournament. Since the game was just on the other side of town, we did not bus as a team to the game. I told the players to arrive at the Bloomington High School parking lot across from the baseball field by 3:15 p.m. and, as was our tradition for a road game, we would walk to the field as a team.

I had not provided any instructions on wearing the "MCstrong – We Believe" shirts I had passed out at practice. Given the cross was prominently and proudly displayed on the front, and the message of the Christian song, I thought it might be best not to wear them.

I arrived at the parking lot around 2:45 pm. A few moments later the players started arriving. Some of them were by themselves. Others arrived in pairs.

Every single one of them had on their new, bright gold, "We Believe" shirt.

All players were present and accounted for by 3:15. Conversation was fairly limited as the players began to congregate in the lot. The relative quiet as this team of teenage players gathered may have been a signal of increased focus on this potentially one and done game.

Of course, it may also have been due to heightened nerves at what could be the last game of the season.

"We have everything?" I asked.

I took silence as an affirmative.

"Let's go," I said.

Our first round opponent, the Lincoln High School Railers, had not arrived yet, nor had any spectators. One person was setting up at the gate to take tickets, and another person was preparing the field. Otherwise the park was empty.

We quietly walked across the road and up the paved path leading to the baseball field.

I walked behind this group of warriors. The afternoon sun was beaming down from a cloudless sky, making the bright gold shirts seem to illuminate.

No one was there to see this band of brothers arrive in their gold shirts – shirts pronouncing remembrance of Michael, their hope in God, and their belief in each other.

Had anyone been there to watch us enter, they would have seen my pride beaming brighter than the sun.

Lincoln had a baseball history steeped in tradition and success. They also had the advantage of beating us in a regular season game just two weeks ago, providing them a critical confidence boost. We had lost that game at Lincoln 11-8, but our players were smart enough to know the game wasn't as close as the score appeared.

Lincoln's confidence was on full display as they got off the bus and entered the field with what seemed to me a definite swagger, sporting red and green camouflage jerseys. I assumed the gaudy shirts were just for pregame show, but it soon became clear that it was their game attire.

As our guys went through the pregame ritual of stretching exercises and throwing, I taped the lineup chart to the dugout wall and then scanned the Bloomington High School baseball field.

Since we share a home field with the Illinois State University baseball team, the U-High varsity baseball team had grown accustomed to practicing and playing on a pristine, well-manicured field. Two years ago the University installed field turf on the infield, reducing the potential for rainouts and eliminating bad hops on the infield.

We were spoiled.

We certainly loved and enjoyed our beautiful home field, but taking most of our ground balls in practices on the field turf carpet could actually be a competitive disadvantage when we played on infield surfaces ranging from less-than-perfect to outrageously bumpy.

This BHS field was on the outrageously bumpy end of the scale.

Our guys had played enough games on this field over the years to know it.

The pitchers mound was no doubt several inches higher than the rule book allowed, and every player and coach in town knew it. But every year the mound seemed to be an inch higher.

The infield "dirt" was actually a crushed limestone. So to say it was hard as rock was a completely factual statement. It may have absorbed water to help prevent cancellations, but it could be extremely unfriendly to infielders.

The grass on the infield gave an illusion of acceptability, but it actually covered a variety of bumps and imperfections that could turn any ground ball into a bad hop single, or worse yet, a bad bruise on an unsuspecting infielder.

As we took our pregame infield and outfield warm-ups, I could sense a nervousness and hesitancy I hadn't seen in this team for several games.

The infielders were very hesitant, seemingly expecting a bad hop on everything hit their way.

I also sensed frayed nerves even beyond the normal concerns in preparing for a game knowing the season comes to an end with a loss.

As we finished our pregame infield and outfield routine, I gathered the team at the end of the dugout for a quick meeting.

Eighteen sets of eyes were on me as I gathered my thoughts. Something told me I needed to give them permission to fail.

"Who can tell me what our record is?" I started.

Travis Auer was quick with the answer.

"22-12," he said.

"That's 34 games. This isn't the first game of the regional tournament. It's just game number 35. All I ask of you each and every game is that no matter what your role is for that game, you give that role everything you have to give. You perform your role to the absolute best of your ability. That was my expectation the first game of the season, and the 10th game of the season, and the 25th game. That's all I've ever asked. No more. No less.

Did you guys play hard in the first game of the season?

Heads nodded.

Did you play hard in the 10th game of the season?

Heads nodded again.

Did you give me everything you had in game 25?

Heads still nodded.

This game isn't any different than the first 34. It's just game 35.

You don't have to try any harder. You don't have to focus more. You don't have to play with more energy. You don't have to play with more enthusiasm. You just have to play hard like you've played the first 34 games. This is just game 35.

We good?

Heads still nodded.

OK. Last thing. We know the field isn't great. The infield has some bad hops. I don't want to hear another word about the field. We've attacked ground balls on defense all year, and we are going to keep attacking them today. There will be some bad hops. We will make some errors. The key is not letting one error turn into two. We will have adversity today. You guys have overcome adversity all year, and you will overcome any adversity that gets thrown at us today. Remember, the most important pitch is always the next pitch.

It's just game number 35. Relax and play hard.

Get a couple more sprints in and get ready to go."

Deciding on starting pitchers is a very crucial decision in a one-and-done format like the IHSA baseball state championship tournament. Some coaches take the one-game-at-a-time approach and start their ace in game one. Other coaches look at potential opponents, and often start their second best in game one of the regional knowing, at least on paper, a higher seed and tougher matchup lies ahead in the championship game.

Given what we had been through, I decided any tournament win would be a blessing to this group and sent our best available pitcher, junior Kyler Ummel, to the hill.

It appeared Lincoln had decided to save their best pitcher for the championship game. I mentioned that to our team as we took the field.

Ummel retired Lincoln's tough leadoff hitter on a pop up to start the game, but then walked the next batter. After a ground out for the second out, the Lincoln runner tried to steal second. Sophomore catcher Zach Frey threw a laser to second base. Nick Mosele was waiting with the ball for the runner. Inning over.

Zach Frey was an undersized sophomore with a big arm. He started the season as a backup catcher to junior Zach Falasz. If talent is reasonably comparable, I've always believed in giving seniors first shot ahead of juniors, and juniors ahead of sophomores. As the season wore on however, it became clear Frey was better behind the plate and had a superior arm. He also added speed to the lineup. We eased the talented sophomore into the starting lineup, and made the decision he would be our catcher in the postseason.

Zach Falasz handled this transition with unbelievable grace. He gave his best effort when he played, and supported his teammates from the dugout when he wasn't playing. That is not an easy thing for a 17 year old who was the starting catcher at the beginning of the year to do, and said a lot about Zach Falasz and what this group was all about.

Zach Falasz was the first person out of the dugout to greet Zach Frey as we sprinted off the field.

Being the first team to score in a baseball game can be a big factor in who wins, and it takes on added significance in a win-or-go-home post-season game. We jumped on top in textbook fashion.

Speedy Bryan Russell led off with a walk and promptly stole second base. Tyler May hit a ground ball to the right side just like every coach teaches, moving Russell to third. Bryan got a great jump and scored when Ummel grounded out to the third baseman, giving the Pioneers a 1-0 lead after the first inning.

The lead didn't last long.

After getting the first out, Ummel surrendered a hard hit double and back-to-back singles that put Lincoln ahead 2-1. After an error by Kendall Warner, Lincoln had two runners on, and we had the dreaded big inning we talked about staring us in the face.

Ummel got a strikeout and fly out to end the inning with the Railers ahead 2-1. It stayed that way until we came to bat in the bottom of the 3rd inning.

Responding to challenges and overcoming adversity are the marks of any champion.

A 2-1 deficit really didn't represent much adversity to this group. And we responded in a big way.

Tyler May tied the game with a line drive single to rightfield. Ummel reached on an error, and a hit-by-pitch loaded the bases. McLean Conklin laced a single to center, putting us ahead 4-2.

We weren't done.

Kendall Warner drove in a run with a sharp single to right, making it 5-2. A wild pitch followed to make it 6-2 as Lincoln unraveled. Zach Frey singled in a run to make it 7-2, and the Lincoln coach finally decided to put in his best pitcher.

It was too late.

Another wild pitch made it 8-2. May drove in two more runs with a booming double to make it 10-2, and Ummel joined the hit parade with an RBI single for the 9th run of the inning and an 11-2 lead.

As the inning ended, I met Kyler Ummel as he left the dugout to head back out to the pitchers mound.

"We need to bring that momentum back into the dugout with us," I reminded Kyler. "You need to throw another goose egg at them this inning and then we will put them away."

"Will do Coach," he responded confidently.

He backed it up with a 1-2-3 inning, a fly out sandwiched between two strikeouts.

The offense then held up its end of the plan, tacking on four more runs. Conklin led off with a double and scored on a Warner single. Junior Ryan Scott drew a walk. Frey doubled in Warner and Scott, then later scored on a wild pitch making the score 15-2, and we coasted home from there for a 16-6 win.

Following the post-game handshakes, I headed out toward left field to meet with the team. As was our custom, all players were on one knee awaiting my remarks.

There were certainly smiles and laughter, but I was surprised to find the group relatively subdued after such a convincing tournament victory.

It was clear they had a bigger mission in mind.

> "I've never been more proud of a team in my life. You guys have been through a lot this year. You got behind 2-1 today and didn't bat an eye.
>
> There is no doubt in my mind those guys thought they would walk all over us today. They came out strutting around in those ugly red and green camouflage jerseys.
>
> You guys showed them what this baseball team is all about. You played hard. Every pitch. Every play. Every at-bat. We had all kinds of great hustle plays. Our bench was great the whole game.
>
> But you know what I like best about winning today?
>
> It means I get to practice with you guys at least two more days!
>
> I love you guys.
>
> Break it out and I will see you at practice tomorrow."

As I walked back toward the dugout with the rest of the coaches the players huddled together.

"One, two, three – MC!" I heard them chant.

My eyes welled with tears.

CHAPTER 33

• • • • • • •

You Were Meant To Do This

We were expecting to play crosstown rival and top-seeded Bloomington if we made it to the championship game.

Bloomington had the best pitcher in the regional field, a hard-throwing right-hander that attracted Division I college coaches to Raider games all spring. They decided to save him for the championship game, starting their second best pitcher against the 4th seeded Canton Little Giants.

Canton upset the host and top-seeded Raiders 3-1.

It felt like another piece of the puzzle might have just fallen into place.

We had a great two days of practice between our game one win and the championship game scheduled for Saturday. We had extended the season and I wanted to prove to our guys I meant what I said about getting two more days of practice with them.

We took a lot of swings. We took a lot of ground balls. We worked on our bunt game. Our pitchers threw some light bullpens. We reviewed some defensive situations to make sure we were prepared.

But mostly we had fun.

We cranked up the music several decibels during batting practice. We let the kids wear shorts as warmer spring weather had arrived. We kept a great balance between focus and fun.

You could feel the special bond that had wrapped itself around this group. It was clear we all enjoyed being together as a team for two more days.

While the team had fun, I fretted about who would pitch the championship game. Ummel told me he would be ready, but he certainly couldn't start on two days rest. We really weren't certain who our number two was at this point.

While I worried about this crucial choice, it also dawned on me I felt an unusual peace about making this decision.

For the first season I could remember, in over 20 years of coaching, both as an assistant coach and head coach, not a single parent had complained about playing time decisions - at least not directly to any coach.

I would like to think my "one team" preseason pep talk had finally made a difference, but more likely it was the parents realizing any concerns about playing time or lineup decisions were extremely petty and shallow given what I had suffered through, and wisely opted to keep any concerns to themselves.

Regardless, it was a very welcome change.

I lay awake contemplating the pitching decision. It had been such an unusual season. Different times call for different thinking. We considered Ummel our best, but we simply did not have a clear shutdown number one guy with a big arm like most good high school baseball teams need for a postseason run.

So this year we would have to think differently. We would look more closely at matchups. If we couldn't overwhelm them with one guy, we would keep them off balance with more than one.

Decisions to keep pitchers in, or take them out, were always difficult. Conventional wisdom always seemed to error on the side of staying with your best. This year I decided if I was going to error it would be on the side of making a change too quickly, rather than too late.

Coach Paxson suggested sophomore Jon Rink as the championship game starter. He did have the lowest earned run average on the team, but he had only pitched 22 innings. He didn't really figure much into our pitching plans when the season started, but he had a good arm and a high baseball IQ. We started using him in relief an inning or two at a time, and he kept having success every time we sent him out there.

But could we really start a sophomore, who had only started one game on the mound all season, in the regional championship game?

That is just not supposed to happen.

A different season calls for thinking differently.

Jon Rink would be our starting pitcher for the championship game.

We planned to meet as a team again on Saturday morning in the parking lot across the street from the baseball field. Once again, our players arrived one by one. Once again, all the players wore their gold shirts; "MCstrong" on the front; "We Believe" on the back.

We gathered together and prepared to cross the street as a team.

I stopped them.

> "Before we head over I want to read you something. You know how much I love the book "Dare to Be Uncommon" by Tony Dungy. It will always have a very special place in my heart. He also wrote a daily devotional to go with the book, and for two years I read it every single day. I gave a copy to Michael and he had been reading it every day too.

The day we were getting ready to play for the state championship two years ago, this was the daily devotional. It was perfect for that day. We took batting practice at Illinois Central College and I read this to the team before we headed over to O'Brien Field for the championship game.

I know we aren't getting ready to play for a state championship, but I remembered this devotional when I woke up this morning and I wanted to share it with you. Please listen to this message.

The daily devotion is titled "Letting God Fight."

It is based on Exodus 14: 13-15.

The scripture reading from Exodus says, "Moses told the people, don't be afraid. Just stand still and watch the Lord rescue you today. The Egyptians you see today will never be seen again. The Lord himself will fight for you. Just stay calm. Then the Lord said to Moses, "Why are you crying out to me? Tell the people to get moving!"

Here is what Dungy writes for the daily devotional.

"Sometimes we get too caught up in the moment.

Or, more precisely, we get too caught up in our supposed ability to *control* the moment.

Mike Martin, the head baseball coach at Florida State, has been wildly successful in four decades at the school, becoming one of the three winningest college baseball coaches ever. He has gone to the College World Series thirteen times, even though he would note he is still looking for his first championship.

Not too long ago, on a recent trip to the College World Series in Omaha, Nebraska, he texted this response to a well-wisher: "Exodus 14:14. Letting God fight for me."

We always strive for what's best. Coach Martin pushes himself and his team for whatever is on the next horizon, and that's the right response. After all, you're where you are for a reason. Don't quit or mail it in. God doesn't ask Christians to be soft, weak, or passive. If you're a great saleswoman, close the deal. If you're a great attorney, win the lawsuit. If you're a great coach, win the game.

But don't leave the earth scorched behind you in the process. Don't let your stress level grow. You can't control everything. You can prepare only up to a point, as Moses did, and then you have to step back and say "I've done enough'. The Lord himself will fight for me. Just stay calm.

Just stay calm. It's tough to do, but how liberating it is when we realize that it doesn't ultimately fall on us. When Coach Martin runs up against those tough moments, those bad calls, he takes a deep breath and looks for God's peace. A peace that comes in knowing that God works along side us, through good times and bad times.

And that he will always fight for us.

The Lord himself will fight for you. Just stay calm. Believe that the ultimate outcome in whatever you are facing is in the Lord's hands."

I want you guys to stay calm today. Some good things will happen and I have no doubt some bad things will happen. No game is ever perfect. No team is ever perfect. And you won't be perfect today. But no matter what happens, stay calm. Trust. Believe.

Let's go."

We crossed the street and headed down the path leading to the field, our gold shirts once again glistening in the bright sunlight of a glorious morning. In the most soothing voice I could muster, I had told them to stay strong, but my stomach was churning.

I wanted to win every game I've ever been a part of, but this one felt different.

This band of brothers walking in front of me deserved some kind of championship more than any team I've ever known.

I was even more focused than usual on all the tasks leading up to the game. Getting the lineup posted on the dugout wall. Making sure the hitting and pitching charts are ready. Getting my note cards prepared.

Making sure I had a plan in mind and on my note cards for pitching options, pinch-hitting options, and potential defensive changes.

We took our pregame outfield and infield practice routines, and then watched intently as Canton took theirs. It was a chance to scout the strength of arms in the outfield. To see what kind of arm their catcher possessed. To see how athletic the third baseman was and if we could bunt for base hits. Before I knew it, it was time for the pregame meeting with the umpires.

As I turned from my coaches meeting with the umpires at home plate and headed back toward the dugout, I realized there were far more people at the game than I expected. I spotted the usual parents and family members seated in the small section of aluminum bleachers behind home plate, but paused ever so slightly in surprise as I saw the large gathering of spectators lined up past our dugout down the left field line.

Scanning the throng of people, some standing and some in lawn chairs, extending out from our dugout and well past the bullpen located on the left field foul line, it dawned on me this had become something more than a high school baseball regional championship game.

I spotted Kelly in a lawn chair just on the other side of our dugout. Jimmy and my nephew Jon were standing next to her. Jimmy was wearing a U-High jacket.

Standing near them was a group of Michael's best friends and high school baseball teammates; Jason Cullen, Jacob Birlingmaier, Tyler Emmerson and Brad Hallstein.

A little further down the line I spotted Nate Metzger. Next to Coach Metzger stood twins Jacob and Jared Hendren. They were currently playing for Coach Metzger at Heartland after playing on our 2012 state championship team at U-High. Their dad Rusty Hendren, one of my assistant coaches during that state championship season, was with them.

Then I spotted my dad sitting in a lawn chair. Dad was excited when I was named head coach, but I could only remember him being at one other game the last four years just to watch me coach, and he only lasted a few innings at that one.

As I scanned the crowd of familiar faces, it hit me.

They weren't there to see me.

And they weren't there to watch U-High baseball.

They were there because this team represented a connection with Michael we were all so desperate to hang onto.

They were there because my precious son couldn't be.

A waive of emotion struck me. I was light-headed as I reached the corner of the dugout.

I dropped to one knee. I bowed my head.

I had watched proudly all season as our players huddled before every game for a team prayer. Personally though, I had not prayed much in the last couple months as I struggled with my anger towards God and my unanswered prayers in the hospital.

But now, I was overwhelmed.

> "Father God, I miss Michael and I still struggle with what has happened. But I thank you for the 22 years we had with him on this earth. I know this is just a high school baseball game, but these kids have been through a lot. They deserve some happiness. Please watch over them. Help them stay calm. Help them glorify You with their effort. Help me be strong and offer them the right words, wisdom and encouragement. I pray this all in Jesus name. Amen."

We were the home team and prepared to take the field first. I gathered the team in front of the dugout. I wanted to keep the pregame comments brief and purposefully without drama or emotion. I stayed with our now familiar theme.

"Men – this is just game number 36. We aren't going to do anything different than we have done the first 35 games. Just play hard. Every play. Every at-bat. Every pitch. None of those first 35 games were perfect. I guarantee you some things will go wrong today. You will face adversity. Remember the devotional we read in the parking lot. Just stay calm and work through it. Just like we have worked through it all year. It's just game 36."

I told them it was just game 36, but their chant as they broke the huddle reminded me it was something more.

"One, two, three – MC!" they chanted, sprinting onto the field.

Coach Paxson told me Rink looked good in the bullpen and was ready. I watched Jon deliver his seven warm-up pitches. He was around the plate with good velocity and movement. I took a deep breath and began to feel better about starting an untested sophomore in a regional championship game.

He walked the lead-off hitter on five pitches.

Two outs later, the clean up hitter lined a single to left field and we were down 1-0. Another single followed. The next hitter hit a rocket, but right at first baseman Kendall Warner. We were luckily out of the inning, but Canton had struck first.

As our players came off the field I didn't ask them to huddle, but instead fist-bumped and high-fived them and forcefully repeated the same question to each player as they passed me on the way to the dugout.

"How are we going to respond?"

"How are we going to respond?"

"How are we going to respond?"

Leadoff hitter Bryan Russell provided a quick and decisive answer to my question.

With a 1-2 count he drove a fastball deep beyond the center field fence, tying the game at 1-1.

Tyler May singled with one out. McLean Conklin reached base on an error. Ryan Scott was hit by a pitch, and we had the bases loaded with two outs.

We emphasized mental toughness as one of our team's core values. We have always taken pride in scoring runs with two outs because we see it as an indicator of our mental toughness. We had the right guy at the plate.

Kendall Warner had struggled mightily most of the season. He had a lot of bad at-bats, and it seemed when he did put a good swing on a ball he would hit it right at somebody. He found himself on the bench for a few key games while we tried a couple different options at first base. It certainly wasn't how he expected his senior season to go.

But Kendall kept grinding. He took extra swings after practice. He put in extra work off a batting tee. He was clearly a better option for us defensively at first base, so I kept putting him back in the lineup. I thought back to the conversation I had with him before our game at Dozer Field in Peoria.

I remember seeing a look of embarrassment on Kendall's face when they flashed his batting average across the giant video board as lineups were announced before that game. As he headed back to the dugout I stopped him. I put my arm around him.

"You aren't happy about that batting average are you?" I asked.

"No," he responded sheepishly, looking down and pawing at the dirt with his toe.

"Is there anything you can do to change any of those at-bats?"

"No," he replied, now looking up.

"So forget about them," I said. "You are only as good as your next at-bat. Your batting average doesn't mean anything to me. Keep hitting balls hard. I believe in you Kendall. You are our first baseman."

After battling to a 3-2 count, Kendall fouled off a couple tough pitches to avoid a strikeout that would have provided Canton some momentum. He smashed a hard ground ball into left field for a single, scoring two runs and putting us up 3-1. Zach Frey followed with a single to score another run, and the first inning ended with us up 4-1.

How were we going to respond indeed!

Neither team scored in the second inning. Rink walked the leadoff hitter in the top of the third, then got two fly ball outs before walking the next hitter to put two men on with two outs.

I looked down to my note card with pitching options. It read "Quick on the trigger - Don't be afraid to make pitching changes."

Junior Sam Arvik was the next name on the card. Rink had made it through their lineup once. I made the change and put in Sam.

The next batter hit a looping line drive behind second base. It looked like a textbook Texas leaguer, a fluke blooper that would drop in for a single and at least one run.

But second baseman Bryan Russell seemed to appear out of nowhere. His diving catch ended the inning and kept the score 4-1.

Russell led off the bottom of the fourth inning with a walk, and once again stole second base. Tyler May followed with a perfect bunt for a hit and we were primed for a big inning. Two strikeouts followed.

Once again, we faced another two out test. And once again, we had the right guy at the plate.

McLean Conklin had stared down more than his fair share of adversity. Arm troubles had kept him off the field and in a designated hitter role his entire junior season. Those same arm troubles had kept him from pitching, something he loved to do. He had food allergies that kept him from eating the foods all his friends enjoyed and took for granted.

And of course, the loss of Michael had hit him extremely hard.

But McLean persevered. He worked hard to overcome. And he believed.

McLean ripped a deep drive off the wall in centerfield, scoring two runs and giving us a 6-1 lead after four innings of play.

Meanwhile, Arvik kept mowing down Canton hitters. Sam kept throwing ground balls and our defense, anchored by Nick Mosele in the middle, kept making plays. We tacked on a run in the bottom of the sixth and took a commanding 7-1 lead in to the seventh and final inning.

The last three outs always seem to be the hardest to get. I breathed a little easier when the first hitter grounded weakly back to Arik. Two more outs to go.

The next hitter singled, followed by a walk and a passed ball. Another single made it 7-2. Yet another single made it 7-3.

I paced and looked down at my note card. Ummel could probably close, but with a six run lead we had not warmed him up before he went back out to center field. Frey was the next option, but he was catching. We sent left-handed sophomore Jay Burton down to warm up. Burton had spent the entire season with the junior varsity team. He had pitched a grand total of three varsity innings. We really needed Arvik to finish this.

Mosele fielded a routine ground ball and tossed it to Warner. Two down. One more out to go.

I paced some more. As I made my way to the far end of the dugout, I snuck a quick glance toward the spectators still gathered and watching down the third base line.

My dad was still in his lawn chair.

I made my way back to the front of the dugout. I bowed my head and took a deep breath.

"One more Sam," I pleaded.

The next hitter chopped a ground ball towards Kendall Warner at 1B. We held our breath hoping against one of those bad hops common on this bumpy infield.

Kendall fielded it cleanly, and easily beat the hitter to the bag for the third out.

After all the tragedy, and all the heartache, and all the pain, the University High Pioneers were regional champions!

Players sprinted from the dugout and everyone on the field sprinted toward the pitchers mound. The team came together as one in the middle of the field, jumping together in unison and pure joy.

My handshake with Coach Paxson quickly turned into a hug, followed by a hug with Coach Haws. We headed out to home plate and the players broke their celebration to join us for the obligatory postgame handshake line with our opponents.

Ordinarily we would have sprinted into the outfield for a postgame meeting, but instead we stayed at home plate for the championship trophy presentation. The seniors went forward to accept the plaque, and were joined by the entire team as they lifted the plaque over their heads in jubilation for all to see.

A postgame team meeting would have to wait.

Smiling as I watched these kids celebrate with unbridled and well deserved joy, I turned and headed toward my family and friends still gathered down the third base line.

As I reached Kelly, my smile was overtaken by tears. My tears of joy were joined by tears of relief, and pushed aside by tears of sorrow because Michael wasn't here to share this championship with us. I sobbed uncontrollably as she wrapped her arms around me.

"He is with you, and he is proud of you" she comforted me. "He is always with us."

I felt Jimmy's hand on my back as I continued to shake with tears. I pulled him into our embrace. Neither of us spoke, but his squeeze on my back told me he was proud of me, and my squeeze on him told him how happy I was he was here to see it. As we continued our family hug, I heard the gathering of friends and family begin to applaud.

They had cheered for the team following our win, but this was directed at us, acknowledging what we had been through and this brief but fleeting snippet of triumph.

I looked up from our embrace.

I hugged Jimmy's girlfriend Abby, and my nephew Jon. He had been more like a brother to Michael than a cousin, and his tears showed how much he missed him.

I wiped my eyes and made my way over to my dad, now standing by his lawn chair.

Dad was not a hugger, so he reached out his hand as he said "Good job."

I shook his hand but pulled him in close for a hug. I felt his left hand reach around and pat me on the back.

"Thanks for being here dad," I whispered.

My sister Susie was standing nearby. I hugged her tightly.

"Great job," she said. "I love you."

"I love you too," I replied.

Michael's high school friends and teammates were standing close by and I embraced each one.

I saw Coach Metzger waiting. A handshake wasn't even considered as he reached for me with open arms.

"MC is very proud of you today Coach," he said, a quiver in his voice as he choked back tears.

Rusty, Jared and Jacob Hendren were all still there and I hugged each one. Jared and Jacob asked for a picture with me and I was happy to oblige.

As I made my way back toward home plate for team pictures with the championship trophy, I was greeted by Mari Hendren. Mari was the mother of junior Bryce Hendren.

She opened her arms for a hug. As she pulled away she kept one hand on each of my shoulders. Her eyes were moist with tears. She spoke words I will never forget.

"You were meant to do this."

"You were meant to do this."

CHAPTER 34

● ● ● ● ● ● ● ●

A Life Changed

The parents were now gathered on the field with their cameras. We took several team pictures with the regional championship plaque. Players took pictures with other players. The seniors posed together for a shot. Players stood with arms around their parents for family photos, all with the championship plaque proudly displayed, and all with big smiles of a shared joy.

As the pictures were taken, players and parents lingered in groups around the home plate area. There were hugs, tears, smiles, and more hugs. Players, parents, friends, and family stood in groups and recalled highlights and memories from the glorious championship game victory.

We had been through so much together. Nobody seemed to want this moment of joy to end.

Travis Auer decided it shouldn't.

"Hey Coach," he started. "The guys want to go to Buffalo Wild Wings and celebrate."

I paused for a moment.

It had been Michael's favorite place to eat. It was never Buffalo Wild

Wings to him, just "B-Dubs". He seemed to eat there at least once a week. We would often stop after church for wings and fries.

We had not been there since his death.

I was drained. But something told me this celebration needed to continue. Michael's words kept echoing in my head.

More love, more Jesus.

"OK" I agreed. "But we either go as a team or we don't go. All the players need to be there."

He didn't have to twist many arms.

So the victorious regional champions gathered at Buffalo Wild Wings. A few tables were joined together and all the players sat together as one. Kelly and I were at a table nearby with Coach Paxson and Coach Haws. Jimmy and Abby joined us. So did Jon. So did Michael's friends and former teammates – Jason, Jacob, Brad and Tyler.

We had been caught up in the celebration after the game and had not met as a team, so I took a couple of minutes to address them now.

> "I am proud of you guys. I've coached a lot of teams, including a state championship team. I've never been more proud of a group of players. You have gone through things that no high school team should have to go through. I love it that you are regional champions – and I love that I get to spend at least two more days practicing with you guys. The sectional is in Springfield at Sacred Heart Griffin. Mount Zion won today so we will play them on Wednesday night. We will practice Monday at 4:00."

My words did not get a lot of reaction.

The applause came when I told them I would be buying their lunch.

The players enjoyed wings, burgers, fries, and multiple refills of soda. Their conversations were animated and filled with laughter as they celebrated defeating a regional tournament field that included our crosstown rivals.

Conversations were less animated and more varied at our table. We talked about our win and the upcoming sectional tournament, but we also veered often and reminisced about Michael. All of his friends seemed to have a different and favorite story about Michael and Buffalo Wild Wings, and they seemed to enjoy sharing those stories with us.

The bill came and I gave it to Kelly to take care of with our credit card. I told her since we were paying for lunch I would have the players take care of a nice tip for our server. She pulled one of the "Pay It Forward" cards we had created from her wallet.

On the front of the card was a picture of Michael in his Heartland #19 baseball jersey, flashing that precious smile. "Pay It Forward For Michael Collins" was written at the top of the card, and below it the "MCstrong" logo we had created for The Michael Collins Foundation. The MC was capitalized and in a different color, but the power of the logo was in the dramatic cross. The front also included some messages in a smaller font. It read:

> "Michael's life was tragically cut short at the age of 22 by a drunk driver.
> Please, DON'T DRINK & DRIVE.
> We honor God, and Michael's memory, by the kindness you just experienced."

The back of the card included the message Michael wanted everyone to hear. It read:

> "Michael was passionate about many things but the greatest joy he brought his family was his faith in God and his relationship with the Lord. He wanted to help others follow Jesus too. The act of love you just experienced is a simple way to pay it forward – honoring God and Michael's memory through generosity, kindness, and the love of Jesus."

The back also includes Michael's favorite scripture verse – Philippians 4:13.

"For I can do everything through Christ, who gives me strength."

I took the card to Travis Auer and Nick Mosele.

"You guys didn't know I was going to buy lunch, so you should all have money," I started. "Our bill was over $500 and I am very happy to pay it, but you guys need to make sure and take care of our server."

"Will do Coach," Travis replied.

They knew the drill. We had used one of these cards at every road game fast food stop.

But this was not a fast food stop, and the emotion of our championship game win was still gripping their hearts.

I watched as Travis and Nick went around the table, huddling with a few players at a time to discuss their "pay it forward" plans and collect money.

After counting cash and a few more huddles, Travis and Nick came back to me with the card and a wad of bills.

"Is $250 enough Coach," Travis asked.

I swelled with pride. Tears started to swell as well.

"Yes'" was all I could muster in response.

Travis and Nick searched out our server across the room and presented her with the card and the cash.

She looked at Michael's picture and read the card. She knew the story. She had actually served Michael before. Travis and Nick pointed toward our table, letting her know we were Michael's mom, dad and brother.

She briskly walked toward us. Tears streamed from her cheeks. Kelly took a few steps and embraced her.

Two days later a card arrived in the mail, with the following note inside:

> *Kelly & Jim:*
>
> *I'm not really sure what to say or where to start with this letter, so I'll just write it from my heart.*
>
> *I have been touched by the MCstrong acts that I've done and have had done for me.*
>
> *I am so sorry for your loss – Michael. He loved life and it shows what an impact one young man can have on so many people. As I look around I can now see why he lived the way he did, with you both as his examples, how could he not? Your strength and love for our Lord shines through with how you have handled such a loss.*
>
> *I wanted to share with you both what an impact you had on my daughter (your Buffalo Wild Wings server) the day you won the regional with U-High.*
>
> *It was not the money the boys left but the MCstrong card and your kind hugs you shared with her that day. She could see your pain but also your strength and grace that God alone can give us all.*
>
> *She is hurting and has fallen away from church. As a college second year student she is lonely, lost, confused.*
>
> *You both taking the time to hug and encourage her really touched her. She called her dad and me and was overwhelmed.*
>
> *Kelly, I've done Bible Study Fellowship with you a few years back and remember your sweet personality. Thank you both for giving us all an example to live by.*
>
> *Love and God's Blessing to you,*

I read the letter and thought yet again of Michael's words; more love, more Jesus.

Only God.

CHAPTER 35

● ● ● ● ● ● ● ●

House Money

Sacred Heart Griffin would play host to our IHSA sectional tournament. SHG was a private school located about 75 miles south of Bloomington-Normal in the state capital of Springfield, Illinois.

The school proudly displayed all the trappings of wealthy donors and alumni, including a campus full of beautiful brick buildings. Both the football and baseball fields were lighted and covered in bright new field turf, with video scoreboards and brick concession stands that would make any college athletics program proud.

Since we played all our home games on field turf, we weren't concerned about playing on a different surface.

Then we found out there would be a difference.

We had worn the same metal-cleated baseball shoes on both our home field turf and the more typical dirt and grass fields on the road.

We were informed Sacred Heart Griffin does not allow metal-cleated shoes on their field turf.

Trying to leave no stone unturned, we told our players they needed to have non-cleated shoes for practice on Monday. Some purchased new shoes with plastic-molded cleats. Others showed up in football shoes and soccer shoes. There was a lot of grumbling in the dugout about the home team rule as the players changed their shoes and prepared for practice.

I gathered the team in front of the dugout before they headed out to warm up. I wanted to keep it light but make a point.

"I hear a lot of grumbling about the shoes. Believe me guys, I understand. When I played I was extremely particular about how I looked. Does that surprise you? Now you know why we have three different jerseys! And I'm not gonna lie – if I had to wear a different pair of shoes than what I wore all year I wouldn't be happy about it. And you know it's not easy for me to see so many different colors of shoes on the same team! But we need to control what we can control. This is a rule and we follow rules. We have to keep this in perspective. Is this really going to be the kind of adversity that bothers us? Seriously? After what we've been through, are we really going to let this bother us? I don't think so. I don't want to hear any more about shoes. You have two days to practice in them. I guarantee you if we lose tomorrow it won't have anything to do with our shoes!"

The players nodded in agreement. With the regional championship under our belt, I also wanted to make sure these guys continued to enjoy the ride.

"I know you guys don't gamble but if you did, you would know what the term "house money" means. I'll make it simple. You place a bet. If you win the bet you put the original money in your pocket and start betting just the money you won on your bet. You are playing with house money.

Guys, we are playing with house money. As you advance in the tournament the tendency is to feel more pressure. We shouldn't feel any more pressure. We should feel less pressure. We have already accomplished far more than anyone thought we would.

Are you kidding me? Two of our best pitchers haven't been able to pitch all season. We had to play through a tragedy tougher than most people could possibly imagine. We didn't win our conference. Nobody thought we would win our regional.

But we did!

I'm tellin' you guys, you shouldn't feel any pressure. We are playing with house money!"

We had another relaxed and fun practice. We also had a few extra visitors watching us work out.

Our advancement into the sectional tournament captured the attention of the local press, as they sensed another feel-good story rising from the ashes of this senseless tragedy.

Randy Kindred had devoted two or three of his columns in the Daily Pantagraph to our tragedy after Michael's death, and his inspiring words had helped bring some healing to our family and the community.

He stopped by practice for a follow up visit with our team, and his column on the front page of the sports section the following day helped remind us of our bigger mission.

Kindred: Michael Collins still guiding U High players

Don't expect it to happen every time Tyler May is in the batter's box.

He doesn't.

Yet, he knows it will happen when he needs it most. There is comfort in that.

A University High School senior, May realizes he occasionally might succumb to an old habit…allowing his hands to drop and his bat to drift.

That's when the familiar words of Michael Collins will intervene.

"He was really big on making sure I had my hands up and getting the bat right through the zone instead of casting out a bit," May said. "Definitely, I'll be hearing his voice."

It is among the many things May and his teammates carry with them from Collins, the 22-year-old assistant coach who died in April from injuries suffered in a car accident. The son of head coach Jim Collins was an inspiring and trusted member of the Pioneers.

A former infielder at Normal West High School and Heartland Community College, the younger Collins had credibility and a connection with U-High players.

"We bonded," May said. "We were all pretty close with him. He had been where we are, he knew what we're going through."

As Jim Collins said recently, "Our players tolerate me. They loved Michael. He was their age. He was the cool one."

So last Saturday, as the Pioneers captured the regional championship with a win over Canton, they could feel Michael Collins' presence… in how they threw across the diamond, how they swung the bat, the way they tucked their jerseys in.

Everything was done with a purpose.

Junior Nick Mosele and his teammates were heeding Collins' words, as surely as if he was there next to them.

What did they hear?

"Make sure if you're going to do anything, you're doing it correctly," Mosele said. "Make sure that you master the skill of anything you're trying to do."

"It's amazing how Michael's legacy can like…live on," Sam Arvik said. "For example, the Pay it Forward for Michael, that's exactly what he would want us to do with that."

This is a team that has gained strength from facing the unthinkable together. The players have also received support from others.

"I've had a lot of friends from junior high and elementary school really reach out to me," Mosele said. "I've had a lot of former teachers and especially family members contact me, making sure I'm in good health and doing OK."

"No one could have expected this to happen," said junior Zach Falasz. "Everyone coming around and rallying around us has been special, especially parents and coaches."

"We are finishing up the season right, and we're doing it for Michael."

CHAPTER 36

• • • • • • •

One Team

The column served as a wonderful reminder of what this team had suffered through together, and the mission we were on. They used hushed tones, but several players discussed the column as we prepared for practice on Tuesday.

As the players prepared for yet another extra day of practice, I continued to wrestle with a decision on who should be the starting pitcher. The most logical answer seemed to be stick with a "one-game-at-a-time" approach and start Kyler Ummel in game one of the sectional, just as we had for the regional.

But nothing about this season was logical.

Beating either Champaign Central or Sacred Heart in the championship game would be improbable at best, and nearly impossible without several innings from our best pitcher. In fact, beating either of them would probably require a mix of at least our top four pitchers being available.

But that would mean doing something crazy – like starting our fourth or fifth best option in game one, hoping to have enough of our best arms left to give us any kind of a shot in the sectional final.

Huddled alone with the coaches in the dugout before practice while the players warmed up in the outfield, I decided to discuss my crazy idea.

"What do you think about starting Galindo tomorrow?" I started.

Austin was a hulking 6'6, 215 pound sophomore man-child. As a freshman last year he threw harder than anyone at tryouts. We gave him a place on the varsity roster and expected to harness his size and velocity, making him a significant contributor on our pitching staff.

It didn't happen.

He could either throw hard with absolutely no command, or throw with some command but scaled-back velocity.

He showed some flashes of brilliance during the summer, so we couldn't wait to see him blossom into one of our best pitchers during this, his sophomore season.

We were still waiting.

No matter how much time he spent with Coach Paxson watching video and doing drills to improve his mechanics, Austin just could not get that big body in sync.

He showed us an occasional flash, but the only thing consistent with his pitching was his inconsistency in throwing strikes.

Early in the season we were determined to keep running him out to the mound and let him figure it out, but eventually we decided progress would have to be made in the bullpen rather than in a game.

He pitched in six games and started four during the season, but only ended up with 13 innings pitched. He walked 19 in those 13 innings.

But his best five innings were the last five innings he pitched, in the second game of a doubleheader the last Saturday of the season against Rock Island. Those five innings reminded us of his potential and the hopes we had for this giant.

Hence, my crazy idea to start him against Mount Zion.

"You mean in the outfield?" Coach Haws asked.

"No, I mean the starting pitcher," I chuckled.

Their startled looks told me they agreed on one thing – the idea was crazy.

"Why not Ummel," Coach Paxson said.

"I think we need him to have any chance in the championship game," I responded.

"I agree, but what about Arvik or Rink," he countered.

"I think we might need them in the second game too," I replied.

"We can't win the second game if we don't win the first one," Coach Haws reminded us.

"Austin threw well the last game he pitched against Rock Island," I countered.

"Mount Zion isn't Rock Island," Coach Paxson responded.

I was in the dugout watching batting practice and my mind wandered back to the first game of the regional tournament in 2012, the year we won the state championship. The coaches wanted to save our dominant ace for the championship game of the regional.

Most years I may have agreed with them, but in my mind that team had the potential to win the whole thing. And the rotation to give us the best chance at reaching the state finals and winning a state championship would be to have our ace pitch game one of the regional and sectional, making him ready for the super-sectional game that would determine a berth in the state tourney final four.

That decision turned out pretty well when our ace threw a no-hitter in the super-sectional and seven strong innings in winning the state championship game.

I remembered talking to that team about our pitching strategy, wanting them to hear that I was planning to win a state championship, not just one game.

I met with Austin just as practice was wrapping up. He had to be shocked by this news, but he didn't show it. The players gathered and stored all the equipment, then changed their shoes. We huddled on the field just outside the dugout.

"Men, we don't know who we will play in the championship game – but we know it will be one of the best teams in the state. Champaign Central is 35-2. Sacred Heart Griffin is 34-3. The Prep Baseball Report says they are two of the best teams in the State – in any class.

Don't get me wrong – I think we can win this thing. But I do think we have to think a little differently and be creative in order to put us in a position to win this sectional championship.

If we were only worried about beating Mount Zion and nothing else, we would start Kyler. He's our number one right now and he's ready to go.

But we're playing with house money. I'm not looking for just one win.

I'm looking for you guys to shock the world!

Our best chance to win a sectional championship is to have plenty of arms available on Saturday so we can mix and match against either Champaign or Sacred Heart. That means we have to think a little differently tomorrow.

Austin is going to be our starting pitcher. His last time out he gave us five good innings against a very good Rock Island team. We don't need Austin to give us a complete game – just a few good innings. And he is going to do that.

That will put us in a position to get the win tomorrow, and then shock the world on Saturday.

Are you with me?"

I watched them very closely to guage their reaction.

There was no doubt several pitchers might think they were more deserving to start this crucial game. Several might think they were more qualified to start. Most of the team would have expected somebody other than Austin to be the starting pitcher tomorrow.

This group was smart with plenty of baseball savvy. There is no way they heard that announcement and didn't think the idea was, at best, a little nuts, and at worst, the dumbest decision ever made by a baseball coach at any level.

I watched their eyes and actions closely.

They had a special look in their eyes.

Their eyes stayed focused on me, telling me they trusted me to make the right decisions.

Each and every one of them seemed to be processing the announcement and immediately determining what they could give to help the team.

Their actions confirmed my hopes.

They began to encourage Austin with hoots and hollers, patting him on the back and showing nothing but confidence in him.

I smiled.

We were ONE TEAM!

"Michael would be so proud of you guys," I said.

"Let's break it out - team on three," I offered.

"MC on three," Travis Auer corrected me.

"One, two, three – MC!" they chanted.

As they broke their huddle and left the stadium, I could only think of one thing.

God bless them.

CHAPTER 37

● ● ● ● ● ● ●

Sweet 16

Our bus pulled onto the spacious Sacred Heart Griffin campus around 5:00 pm for our 6:30 game. If our kids didn't play their football and baseball home games in the Division I college stadiums at Illinois State, they most likely would have been in awe of this sprawling athletic facility.

I had to remind myself this was a high school campus.

It appeared about the only thing the school wasn't prepared for was seating around the baseball field when the two best teams in the state are playing each other in the sectional tournament opener!

Sacred Heart Griffin beat Champaign Central 2-0, which meant two things; we knew we would play SHG if we won, and most of the overflow home crowd would be staying to watch our game.

We had begun our stretching and warm ups on the football field, and now made our way as a team down the paved path leading from the football field to our dugout on the third base side. The crowd was still several people deep along the foul line, forcing us to go single file through the throng. The buzz from the epic first game battle was still creating an electric energy around the field.

All I could think of was how happy I was for these kids to get to play in this kind of environment.

And how much I wished Michael could be walking through this crowd with me.

I finished my meeting with the umpires and turned, heading to our standard pregame huddle. The players were still down the foul line, all on one knee with heads bowed, in their pregame prayer ritual. They broke and headed toward me.

Our huddle was once again short and sweet, intended to calm them down not fire them up, once again relying on some now familiar themes.

"House money fellas. You are here – nobody expected that from you. Our season is already a success. There is no pressure to win. You are already winners. This is just game number 37. Just play hard and leave no regrets on the field. Remember – things will go wrong. We will face adversity – but nothing we can't handle. Always focus on the next pitch. Let's get 'em early!"

We broke the huddle and got ready to hit.

Bryan Russell led off with a line drive. It was misplayed by the right fielder and Bryan sped all the way around to third. Tyler May struck out, followed by a walk to Kyler Ummel. Galndo popped up on the infield for the second out.

Here we were again, another of what we referred to as "mental toughness moments." Runners are at the corners with a chance to jump on top. It's a hugely critical opportunity to grab momentum and a chance to challenge their spirit with a two out RBI.

And once again we passed the mental toughness challenge.

McLean Conklin ripped a single to right field, putting us on the board with a 1-0 lead. Ryan Scott followed with another single to right, and we took a 2-0 lead after one half inning.

Coach Paxson took his seat on a bucket at the dugout entrance nearest home plate, preparing to signal in pitches to catcher Zach Frey.

"How did Austin look in the bullpen coach," I asked.

"Be prepared to get somebody ready in a hurry," he bluntly replied.

We watched together as Austin took his allotted seven warm up pitches. By my estimation, had his seven warm up pitches counted, the lead-off hitter would have walked and the second hitter would have a 3-0 count.

It actually crossed my mind to get somebody throwing in the bullpen before the first official pitch of the game.

Instead, I said a silent prayer and shouted words of encouragement, doing my absolute best to show nothing but the utmost confidence in Austin to throw strikes and get people out.

The leadoff hitter and his coaches had watched what I watched, so of course he took the first pitch – strike one! He hit a ground ball to Kendall Warner at first base on the second pitch for the first out.

The second hitter also took the first pitch – strike one! Then he took the second pitch – strike two! He grounded to Rink at third base for the second out.

The third hitter swung at the first pitch and punched a lazy fly ball to Ummel in center field – three up, three down!

We went down harmlessly in the top of the second inning, and Austin jogged back out to the mound. He seemed to have a different bounce in his step after his perfect first inning. His warm up pitches were around the zone with some life on them, and my heartbeat edged at least a little closer to a normal game rhythm.

It started back up when the count went to 3-1 on the first Mount Zion hitter. I held my breath as Austin came through with a strike and coaxed a weak ground ball to second base. One away.

The second hitter swung at the first pitch – God bless him – and flied out to right field. The third hitter of the inning took a strike before lifting another lazy fly to right, easily caught by Tyler May.

Six up – six outs!

My heartbeat slowed a little further. The idea of needing somebody ready began to fade.

Kyler Ummel led off our half of the third inning with a booming double to the gap in left-center field, and one out later McLean Conklin drove a sacrifice fly to deep right field, sending Austin back out to the mound with a 3-0 lead.

The seventh hitter in the Mount Zion lineup led off the third inning, working the count to 2-2. Coach Paxson signaled in a fastball away. Austin unleashed a heater located right on the outside corner – called strike three!

With a 1-2 count on the eighth Mount Zion hitter and Coach Paxson sensing Austin's swelling confidence, a curve ball away was signaled in. In textbook fashion Austin started the ball on the outer third of home plate, spinning it beautifully and leaving it outside the zone when the batter flailed at the sharply breaking pitch. Strike three!

Perfect through eight hitters!

I was certain every parent who had thought before the game that I had lost my mind when I chose the erratic sophomore to start a sectional game, was now hailing me as some kind of baseball genius!

And then – thud!

On a 3-1 pitch Austin hit the ninth place hitter in the ribs.

The next guy walked on four pitches.

"You think we should get somebody up?" I asked Coach Paxson.

"Let's see what this guy does," he replied.

We had got 2 and 2/3 innings trying to pull a rabbit out of our hat with Austin, but now we were getting greedy, wanting him to get us just a little deeper into the game.

With a 3-1 count on the next hitter, we hoped the ship had been righted when Austin threw a strike to make the count full. The next pitch wasn't close – ball four. Bases loaded.

"Sam, go get ready," I yelled to Arvik. "Code red, code red," I added in an effort to convey the urgency.

Coach Paxson walked slowly to the mound to settle down Austin and give Sam some time to get ready.

The very next pitch was smashed into left field, making it 3-1. The good news was the ball was hit so hard the runner on second base couldn't score. The bad news was it was on the first pitch, so Sam wasn't ready yet.

The count went to 3-2 on the next hitter and you could almost hear our large contingent of U-High fans hold their collective breath.

Ball four. It was now 3-2. Bases were still loaded.

I walked to the mound. I pointed to the bullpen and Sam sprinted in. The infielders gathered around us. Austin looked at me dejectedly.

"You keep your head up Austin," I told him. "You did a great job against a great team. You gave us eight outs and we have the lead! You gave us what we needed! Sam is going to get us out of this inning." I patted Austin on the butt as he handed me the ball and jogged off the mound.

Sam threw a first pitch strike and got an easy ground ball to Nick at shortstop, and after three full innings we were clinging to a 3-2 lead.

In the bottom of the fourth, Mount Zion tied the game with a single, a well-executed sacrifice bunt, and a run-scoring double. A hard hit ball up the middle looked like it would give the Braves a 4-3 lead. Shortstop Nick Mosele seemingly came out of nowhere, diving to his left and somehow snaring the grounder and leaping to his feet all in one motion, then throwing a bullet to first base for the crucial third out!

We sprinted off the field tied 3-3, but once again faced adversity as momentum seemed to be swinging in their favor.

By now, anyone thinking this team wouldn't stare down adversity and respond didn't know this team very well!

Russell was hit by a pitch leading off the inning. Tyler May laid down a perfect bunt, moving Russell to second and beating the throw for a base hit. On the next play, Russell stole third, and daringly dashed home when the throw scooted just a few feet away from the shortstop covering third on the throw.

We were back in the lead 4-3!

With nobody out, I started thinking about our pitching down the game's home stretch. Yes we were playing with "house money" and the best case scenario was getting through the rest of the game without using Kyler, but I didn't think about it very long.

"I think we need to get Kyler ready," I told Coach Paxson.

"I agree," he quickly responded.

We were clearly on the same page.

Kyler was playing center field, but with no outs and our team still batting we had time to get him ready in the bullpen. We failed to score further and I decided if we were going to lose this game in the last three innings, it would be with our best guy on the mound. I sent Kyler to the mound for the bottom of the fifth with a 4-3 lead.

We stress to our pitchers and defense the importance of having a shut-down inning after we score.

"Throw a goose-egg at them and get us back in here," I urged Kyler.

He threw four pitches and Mount Zion hit three ground balls. Jon Rink fielded an easy one and Nick made nice plays on two others. We sprinted off the field with a visible energy and confidence.

Ryan Scott reached on an error to lead off the bottom of the sixth. Kendall Warner sacrificed him into scoring position, but Frey flied out.

Once again, we were searching for those back-breaking two out RBI's.

Sophomore Jon Rink walked, and both runners advanced on a wild pitch. An intentional walk followed, bringing Tyler May to the plate.

Bases loaded, two outs. Game on the line. Most high school baseball players would find this to be a tough situation.

Tyler had a different perspective of "tough."

He had watched the good days and bad days as his father, Keith, battled a rare form of cancer over the last four years. Tyler had a tough junior year and his dream of playing college baseball was on hold because college coaches weren't showing any interest. A few short months ago, he stepped up to the free throw line with one second on the clock and his team down one in a regional tournament game against an archrival, and made both shots.

And then he had to show senior leadership when our team experienced the loss of Michael.

Bases loaded and two outs a tough situation?

Tyler took two balls and then laced a booming triple down the right field line, clearing the bases and giving us a 7-3 lead!

We had won seven games in a row, including the two regional wins. During that streak, we had certainly made some occasional errors and mistakes, but we had avoided any real disastrous innings – those innings where multiple miscues pile one on top of the other and usually with dire consequences.

That was about to change.

The hitter for the Braves in their half of the sixth hit a routine ground ball to Russell. The ball bounced off his glove and by the time he recovered it was too late. The next hitter grounded the ball to Rink at third. His throw to second trying to force the runner was wide, and the runner was called safe.

Instead of two outs and nobody on, Mount Zion had two on and nobody out.

High school rules allow three "free" mound visits in a game – trips to the mound without removing the pitcher. Coach Paxson often went out for these free visits to calm the pitcher down.

I decided to use another one now, and I decided I needed to make this visit.

Catcher Zach Frey jogged to the mound from behind the plate, and all the infielders joined us.

You could feel the tension around the mound not uncommon in such a big game, especially when two errors have just been made.

The first thing I did when I got to the mound, was smile. And I kept smiling as I tried to find the right words.

> "What's up? I told you guys some things would go wrong today, didn't I? We're ok. Everybody take a deep breath. Kyler is going to keep throwing strikes and get us another ground ball and we'll make the play. We've got a force at second and third if we need it. OK? That's all I got, but I'm going to stand out here with you until the umpire comes and gets me. Anyone know a good joke?"

It wasn't the first time I had tried to lighten the mood with a joke during a mound visit, but they seemed to be surprised at the request in the sixth inning of a sectional game. Their chuckles told me they had at least relaxed to some degree, but the umpire came out to break it up before one of them could come up with a joke.

The next hitter dribbled a slow roller just out of Kyler's reach. Nick charged hard from his shortstop position and made a great play to nip the hitter at first base for the first out.

I was feeling pretty impressed by the mound visit when Kyler struck the next hitter out, and it looked like we would dodge a bullet.

But the old adage "you can't give a good team more than three outs" is rarely wrong.

And it wouldn't be tonight.

A ground ball to Nick should have been the third out, but it bounced away from him. It was now 7-4, runners on first and third, and the tying run at the plate.

Kyler's next curveball froze the hitter but must have fooled Zach Frey too. The ball skipped off his glove and to the backstop. It was now 7-5.

A ball had not left the infield, but two runs had scored and Kyler had thrown several more pitches in the inning than he should have.

He walked the next hitter. The tying runs were now on base with the go-ahead run at the plate.

I decided to use the last of my "free" mound visits.

Frey jogged back out from behind the plate. The infielders joined us at the mound again. All of us were in the same places as just a few minutes ago, but now it was 7-5.

Kyler was pitching great. We should have five outs but only had two. The primary purpose of this trip was to let him catch his breath after all the extra pitches.

> "Guys, we still have the lead. Don't forget that. Can we do anything about the plays that have already happened? The only thing we are worried about is the next pitch. We just need to get one more out. Jon and Nick, we have a force at third if we need it. Nick, we have a force at second if we need it.
>
> OK, you guys didn't have a joke last time so I have one. Do you remember how to eat an elephant? One bite at a time! This situation may feel like an elephant – so let's eat it one pitch at a time!"

The umpire came out to let me know our meeting had gone on long enough.

Kyler threw a strike on the first pitch to the next Mount Zion hitter. The hitter grounded one a few steps to Nick's left. You could almost feel our fans suck in their breath, perhaps expecting our fourth error of the inning.

Nick fielded it cleanly and flipped to Kendall Warner at first base for the third out.

With one inning left to play we held a 7-5 lead.

Kyler found a seat on the end of the bench. Before I went out to coach third base, I sat down next to him.

"Great job Kyler," I said. "You threw a lot of pitches that inning. How do you feel."

"Great coach," he said. "I've got this."

I believed him.

We went down quietly in our half of the seventh and Kyler headed back out to the mound.

The first hitter flied out harmlessly, but the second hitter lined a single up the middle.

Coach Paxson suggested we get sophomore Jay Burton ready in the bullpen. Jay was a crafty left-hander we had brought up from the JV team late in the season, and he had thrown a couple good innings during the last two games of the regular season.

We sent him to bullpen but I had no intention of bringing him in. We would either win it or lose it at this point with our best on the mound.

Kyler made sure there was no decision needed.

He struck out the next two hitters – and this improbable run would last at least until Saturday!

We were now in the Sweet Sixteen!

As the team gathered for our post-game huddle in the outfield, I knew I would have to keep my comments brief.

I knew tears were close.

And though some of them would be tears of joy, some of them would be tears of grief because Michael was not here to share in this win.

Many times I had cried in front of this team. I knew they would understand why. But tonight I did not want my tears to rain on their joy.

> "Great job men. This was a great team win. Austin gave us what we needed. Sam did a great job in the middle. Kyler closed the door. We got big hits when we needed them. We will keep this short because I'm hungry and we need to get going. Keep in mind, I coached a state championship team just two years ago. I have absolutely never, and I mean never, been more proud of a group of players in my life. I love you guys. We'll start worrying about Sacred Heart tomorrow. Tonight you need to enjoy this. Go talk to your parents and friends. This was a great atmosphere to win a game in. Soak it up – then let's go get something to eat."

Several suggestions on where to stop for dinner were shouted from the back of the bus. Normally I would try everything possible to comply with one of the suggestions.

Tonight I asked the bus driver to find the nearest McDonalds.

It was Michael's favorite place to stop.

CHAPTER 38

• • • • • • •

It's Hard – Compared to What?

The Springfield Sacred Heart Griffin baseball team was a different animal altogether.

After beating Champaign in the first game of the sectional, they were now 35-3.

Even more incredible, twenty-one of those wins were by shutout, shattering the state record.

They had nearly as many shutouts as we had wins!

The Prep Baseball Report, considered the authority on Illinois high school baseball, called them "the best team in the state in any class."

Their talent started behind the plate, with catching phenom Mitch Trees, a 6'2, 200-pound specimen with a sculpted body, big league bat speed, and a cannon for an arm. Trees was committed to play at the University of Louisville, but had just been drafted in the 11th round by the Cincinnatti Reds. He was expected to sign with the Reds as soon as his high school season ended.

Trees hit in the middle of a lineup full of players destined for college baseball. The shortstop was just a junior, but had already committed to play at the University of Notre Dame.

As if their hitting prowess wasn't enough, the pitching staff just simply didn't give up any runs. Their top two pitchers were both headed toward scholarships at Division One schools, and accounted for most of the record setting shutouts.

The Cyclones ace, Connor Ethridge, would take the mound against us. The hard throwing right-hander, headed to Belmont University, had not lost a game all season – a perfect 12-0 with an almost non-existent earned run average.

The Sacred Heart community had rallied behind this powerhouse team destined for greatness, and large numbers of fans poured into the facility well before game time. The mostly black and Vegas gold clad crowd continued to swell as game time approached. The boisterous SHG student section waived signs and rattled various noisemakers.

The number of Pioneer fans in our green and gold paled in comparison to the throng of home team fans, but our parent contingent had arrived early enough to stake out some of the prime seats near our dugout. The small but rowdy group of Pioneer fans did their best to match decibels with the Cyclone faithful.

The numbers and noise gave the park a state championship game feel.

We won the toss and would be the home team. We huddled before taking the field.

> "Is this crowd great or what! You know how many teams in the state of Illinois wish they were playing today? We are so blessed to have an opportunity to play in this kind of environment! Embrace it. Enjoy it. But remember, it's just game number 38! All the pressure is on those guys. Nobody thought we would ever make it this far. They expect to win a state championship. If they lose today, their season will be a disappointment. Not us men – we

are playing with house money! They are good – you guys know that. But remember – we don't have to beat them four out of seven. We don't even have to win two out of three. We only have to beat them once. Nobody in the state thinks we can win. But guess what – none of them matter. You guys know you can win. I know we can win. That's all that matters. Now relax and have fun – let's go make some memories!"

McLean Conklin took the mound for us. Coach Paxson and I felt our best chance, and maybe only chance, was to throw several different arms at them. The plan was to never let any of their hitters see the same guy twice.

When McLean was a junior, we expected him to be one of our top pitchers, but arm issues had kept him from pitching until the last couple weeks of this season. He had shown signs of returning to form in a couple of those late season appearances.

I had wandered around at practice the last couple days having individual conversations with each of our pitchers.

McLean had looked me straight in the eye with utmost confidence, and simply said "I want the ball."

I felt like we needed to get an inning or two from McLean at some point in the game to have a chance, and starting him would insure he had adequate time to warm up.

That was the plan.

If this season had taught us anything it was that life doesn't always go according to plan.

The Sacred Heart leadoff hitter drove a ball deep into left field. Austin Galindo drifted back toward the fence. It looked like he had a beat on it and would make the catch on the warning track. But the ball tipped off the end of his glove, dropping at the base of the fence, and the Cyclones had the leadoff runner on second base.

McLean's next pitch plunked the hitter in the ribs. It was a strange start, and certainly not the one we needed.

It was about to get even worse.

On a 1-2 count, McLean's curveball was low, outside, and in the dirt. Zach Frey dropped to his knees, shifted to his right, and blocked the pitch from getting to the backstop. The runners recognized the pitch would be in the dirt and broke from second and first. The ball bounced off Zach's chest protector and trickled just a few feet from him. He leaped to his feet and grabbed the baseball with his bare hand.

From my spot on the bench, everything seemed to be moving in slow motion.

I wish I could have hit a pause button.

Zach had made a good play to block the pitch, and now wanted to make a great play by throwing the speedy leadoff runner out at third. A little past half way through his throwing motion he saw what everyone else had already seen – he had no chance.

But it was too late. The ball had left his hand. And since he tried to stop his throw, the ball didn't go to third base. It sailed over the shortstops head and into left field. The leadoff runner going to third bounced up from his slide and headed home. The runner going to second sped for third.

And it got worse.

Austin Galindo did what he should as the left fielder – he sprinted to back up third base.

The ball kept rolling all the way to the warning track in left-center.

The runner who started the play at first base kept running and scored without a play.

In all my years playing, watching, and coaching baseball I had never seen anything quite like it.

We were down 2-0 with nobody out.

And we were clearly in a state of shock.

I went to the mound to try and settle everyone down, but we were rattled and the Cyclones smelled blood.

Following another walk and two more errors, I brought in Sam Arvik to pitch. He gave up a single and then got us out of the inning, but it was 4-0 before the top half of the first inning mercifully came to a close.

The swagger and confidence this 35-3 Cyclone team carried before the game soared even further as they excitedly took the field with a 4-0 lead and their ace on the mound. Nobody familiar with high school baseball in the state thought we could compete with SHG, and the smug smiles on everyone wearing black and Vegas gold after the first half inning seemed to say they knew the rout was on.

As we came off the field I decided to gather our shell-shocked group in front of the dugout.

> "Listen up – we're ok guys. The bad news is we're down 4-0 and it's only the first inning. The good news is it's only the first inning! Is being down 4-0 in the first inning hard? Compared to what? How many of you read the Springfield paper today? Their coach said he didn't really know much about us. Guess what – he's about to find out more about us. He's about to find out exactly what this team is made of. Just do what we do. We keep playing hard and we don't quit."

With one out Tyler May reached on an error. Kyler Ummel followed with a single. But Ethridge got a big strikeout followed by a pop up to end the inning. We didn't respond with a score, but putting a couple runners on base was a good signal we didn't intend to go down without a fight.

In the second inning, Arvik got the first out but then gave up a booming double followed by a line shot single. The Cyclones had runners on first and third with their clean up hitter at the plate, menacingly twirling hit bat letting us all know he was ready to blow the game wide open.

Sam had been brilliant for us in relief during the first three post-season wins, but our season hanging in the balance against the top-ranked team in the state would require an entirely different level of mental toughness.

Sam met the challenge head on, freezing the burly clean-up hitter with a sharp breaking slider for strike three and getting the next hitter on a ground ball to Nick at short. Stopping the rally gave us some much-needed momentum as we came off the field.

Kendall Warner started our half of the second inning with a base-hit up the middle. Frey struck out, but Mosele followed with a single into left field.

But Etheridge blew fastballs by Rink for the second out. He seemed to have that rare ability found in great pitchers – the ability to find another gear with runners on base and escape jams and big innings seemingly at will.

He was about to find out our battle-tested warriors had a different gear too.

Bryan Russell crowded the plate, daring Ethridge to throw him an inside fastball he could turn on. He took a pitch on his left shoulder to load the bases.

The raucous SHG fans rose to their feet in unison, clapping and cheering, waiting and expecting to see what they had seen so many times before – Ethridge getting out of an inning unharmed.

Tyler May had other plans.

He shocked the Cyclones and their rowdy fans, driving a fastball deep into the right field corner! Warner and Mosele scored easily, and the speedy Russell motored around third and headed for home.

The SHG second baseman took the relay throw and wisely opted to throw to third base rather than home. Dirt flew as Tyler slid in. He was out on a close play, but not before Bryan had already crossed home plate!

Our U-High fans screamed in delight! The SHG crowed sat in stunned silence. The scoreboard now read 4-3.

Other opponents may have wilted, but these Pioneers had been through too much to just go away.

We had to pinch hit for Arvik in the third inning, so we sent Jay Burton out to pitch in the fourth. His soft tosses from the left side kept the Cyclones off balance and off the board. We came to bat in the bottom of the fifth inning still trailing 4-3.

Etheridge seemed to be getting stronger. It started to feel like time may be running out.

But Tyler May reached on an error by the third baseman, and Kyler Ummel drove a single past the diving shortstop and into left field. All of a sudden we had runners on first and second with nobody out, and the middle of our order up.

Austin Galindo stepped to the plate. The giant sophomore led us in home runs and was capable of launching one over the scoreboard. He also struck out a lot. I decided we at least needed to use one strike to try and bunt the tying run to third and the go ahead run to second.

I flashed the bunt sign.

I yelled a reminder to the runners about their big catcher with the big arm who likes to throw behind runners on the bases. Tyler and Kyler were two of our best base runners. They nodded their awareness.

Etheridge stretched and delivered.

And just like the play in the first inning, everything that happened next seemed to move in slow motion as I watched it unfold from the third base coach's box.

Tyler and Kyler shuffled toward the next base as taught, ready to get a jump if Austin got the bunt down.

The pitch was not only headed off the plate outside, but it was wild high. It appeared to be headed toward the backstop as a wild pitch.

Tyler's view from second base allowed him to anticipate the wild pitch. He took a couple extra shuffles toward third.

Somehow Trees left his feet, reached above his head and across his body to backhand the errant pitch, and in a single motion without hesitation fired a perfect throw to second base.

Tyler never had a chance.

He tried to crawl back in around the tag but was clearly out.

I knew we would fight until the end, but you could sense our last best chance to take a lead and test Springfield with the pressure of playing behind had slipped away.

We stuck to our plan and used three more pitchers to keep them off balance, but the Cyclones tacked on single runs in the 6th and 7th innings to lead 6-3.

We were down to our last three outs.

Bryan Russell singled with two outs, and I wondered if this group might just make one more charge.

But on his 105th pitch of the game, Etheridge caught Tyler May looking for strike three.

And just like that, our season was over.

CHAPTER 39

• • • • • • •

The Last Huddle

We gathered at home plate and went through the customary postgame handshake routine. Normally after a loss, our players would sprint to the outfield after shaking the last opponent's hand.

Travis Auer was the first one in line. He decided this time was different.

As we would only after a win, Travis doubled back to high-five each of his teammates coming through the line. Everyone behind Travis followed suit.

I was last in line. With tears in his eyes, Travis fell into my arms. No words were needed. His hug said it all.

One by one, each and every player hugged me before jogging to the outfield for a final huddle.

I did my best to gather myself as I slowly walked toward the players assembled on the outfield grass.

Most of them were either wiping away tears or trying desperately and unsuccessfully to hold them back.

I knew I would have to keep my comments brief or I would be crying too hard for any of them to understand what I was saying.

"I have never been more proud of a team in my life. They are a very good team, and we gave them more of a battle than anyone in the state expected. You guys have had to deal with something no high school team should have to deal with. I want to thank each and every one of you. I would have never made it without you guys. We are going to hold our heads high as we leave here. Take what time you need. Spend some time with your parents. Then we are going to get on the bus and we are going to find an all-you-can-eat buffet and we are going to stuff ourselves! I want to see the seniors – but let's break it out one more time."

"One, two, three – MC!" they chanted.

I pulled the seniors to the side.

"The rules say I'm not supposed to pray with the team, and I've always tried to obey rules. But you guys have graduated from U-High and you just played your last game, so I would like to pray with you."

We all dropped to one knee, linked arm-in-arm.

"Father God, thank you for the opportunity to coach these young men. I have been so blessed to have them in my life. Holy Spirit please fill them as they go off to college and the next phase of their lives. Give them wisdom and strength Lord as they move on. Guide them and help them make good choices. Help them find their strengths and their gifts and use them for goodness and to advance your Kingdom. Help them lead like Jesus. And thank you God for the time these young men got to spend with Michael the last two years. May his spirit live on within them. I pray this all in Jesus name. Amen."

Players and parents lingered around the field. There were hugs, tears, and reminiscing. It was as if heading to the bus would signify the end of the season, and nobody wanted it to end.

So we lingered.

I found Kelly, Jimmy, and the group of friends and family. They had made the trip hoping to see our run continue, and now they knew

I needed to spend time with the team. I wrestled to keep my emotions in check as I hugged them before they left the park and headed home.

I hugged our Athletic Director and Principal, thanking them for making the trip. I hugged several players again, and then hugged several parents. Eventually the parents headed for their cars and the players headed for the bus.

I stayed behind, gathering my gear, eventually getting my wish and finding myself alone in the dugout.

I sat down on the dugout bench.

I buried my head in my hands and cried.

CHAPTER 40

● ● ● ● ● ● ●

A Message from Michael

I wanted to make sure our annual post-season banquet to honor our players was special – this group deserved it. I also wanted to make sure we didn't deviate from the celebration traditions established four years ago.

We introduced the Freshmen and JV teams. Then I brought up each individual member of the varsity team, one by one, lauding each of them for the role they played, then handing them a varsity letter with a handshake and a hug.

Nick Mosele was presented with our Gold Glove award. Coaches aren't supposed to play favorites, but Nick was no doubt one of Michael's favorites. He had come such a long way from that devastated soul not wanting to take extra ground balls from anyone but Michael, and his defense down the stretch provided a key anchor for our late-season winning streak and tournament run.

Kyler Ummel was presented with our Leading Pitcher award. His brilliant 1-0 shutout at Dozer Park in Peoria gave us confidence and momentum, and his regional win over Lincoln followed by his gutsy three inning save against Mount Zion in the sectional keyed our run to the sweet sixteen.

Tyler May was named our Most Valuable Player. He led us in batting average and big hits, but even more important was the message he sent the team when we asked him to move from shortstop to third base to start the season, and then from third base to outfield a few games in. His selflessness, without hesitation, showed everyone involved in the program what putting the team first looks like.

I wasn't sure if I would address any of this group as head coach again. I was exhausted. I had already asked Coach Haws to take my place with our summer team so I could have a couple months off with no baseball responsibilities.

No matter what my future might hold, I wanted to share some final thoughts with this group of parents and players.

I asked for their patience as I shared some final words: patience because it might take several minutes, and because I would have a hard time getting through it.

> "These last few months have been the worst months of my life. I want to thank everyone in this room for helping Kelly and me get through it.
>
> I want to give a big thank you to Coach Paxson and Coach Haws. This was their first year and they had to step up and play roles they didn't sign up for, but they handled everything thrown their way. We began the season as coaches and through this tragedy became friends.
>
> I want to thank all the parents. You have stepped up in more ways than I could have ever imagined. Your cards and letters mean the world to Kelly and me.
>
> And most of all, I want to thank these players. I wasn't sure I wanted to come back and coach, but getting to see and hug these guys every day gave me a reason to want to get up every day and keep going. You will always have a very special place in my heart.

It's been the worst three months of my life, but in terms of coaching baseball, in some strange ways, it's been the best season of my life. Two years ago we won a state championship, but for what they accomplished both on and off the field, this year's group will always be the greatest team I ever coached.

I still struggle to understand why this had to happen. Why we had to lose Michael. Obviously we have all seen some good come from it. The saved lives from his organ donation. The "Pay it Forward" movement.

But for any of this to make sense, I need to keep seeing more good come from it. So I want to share some lessons I have learned from this team and this season. I want these lessons to live on. I want these lessons to be part of Michael's legacy.

For the last four years, I have tried to instill "One Team" as a core value in this program. I have preached about being unselfish, putting the team before the individual, about how much can be accomplished when coaches, players and parents are pulling in the same direction and putting the team first.

This season has been the closest I have ever been to every single person in a program truly living out that core value.

Players who weren't playing encouraged and supported the players that were and vice versa. Parents sat together rather than in small groups, and they cheered for all the kids not just their own son.

I have been coaching baseball, as an assistant or head coach, for over 20 years. This is the first season I can ever remember not a single parent or player coming to a coach to complain about playing time or coaching decisions.

I'm not naïve enough to think all of you were happy about playing time and agreed with every decision I made. But I believe you all weighed what I, and this team, were going through against any individual concerns and you did what was best for the team.

I think I was a better coach this year. I hugged kids when we won and I hugged kids when we lost. I cared less about winning and losing and more about helping and healing. I focused more on what was going on in their heads and hearts than I ever have before.

This team overcame a horrific and unimaginable tragedy. These kids had to experience things no team should ever have to endure. But we got through it together and exceeded all expectations on and off the field. They emerged from the depths of pain and despair, pulling together to greatness.

I believe all of this was possible because on the morning of March 29th everyone in this room began playing for a purpose bigger than themselves. My hope is that in future years we can accomplish this without a tragedy involved.

There is one more lesson I am convicted to share tonight. I know I am breaking rules here, but if somebody wants to report me and I get fired I can live with it.

We've all heard the words "Game Seven." When we think of Game Seven, we think "do or die," "one and done," "win or go home." But that is not what Game Seven means to me any longer. Game Seven is sitting in a room with Kelly and Jimmy and doctors and our Pastor, singing "How Great Thou Art" and preparing to watch our precious Michael go to be with his Lord and Saviour.

THAT is Game Seven.

And I am so thankful Michael had a relationship with Jesus. And while I struggle with why this had to happen, I trust God has a plan, and good will keep coming from it. My prayer is that anyone in this room who does not have a relationship with Jesus will seek one. And that everyone who does know Jesus, will work to make that relationship stronger.

I want to end by reading you a message from Michael. I promise you these are his words, not mine. Don't think I'm crazy. I will explain when I am done. Just please know this message is directly from Michael.

I looked down, and read aloud the words Michael had written not all that long ago.

"Cry, mourn, think about the good times, then move on and let it change you for the better...Let it give you an understanding that life is too short and can sometimes be cut even shorter.

Once you understand that, live each day as if it's your last because tomorrow isn't promised. Try to live, laugh, and love each day.

Don't ever go to bed without telling your family you love them.

Understand that God has a plan for everyone. He knows every atom of the universe and He knows exactly why things happen and when they do as well.

Each day, just try to move forward and get a little stronger.

Surround yourself with the people you love and make sure you cherish each moment because they won't last forever.

Time heals all wounds. You will get a little stronger each day and things will go back to normal.

I love you and hope this helped…that being said make sure that if you are drinking and ever need a ride please call me or a cab. If you don't have money I will pay for a cab. Be safe. Be smart."

I looked at our players. As tears streamed down my face I tried to bring my thoughts to a close.

"This message, word for word, IS from Michael. It is a text he sent to his friend Sam Nelson almost a year ago when another friend of Sam's was killed in an automobile accident.

Of course, when Michael sent that text he never thought he would be calling Sam on March 29ᵗʰ to give him and his friends a ride home, and that she would become part of our tragedy.

Sam and two other girls were in the car with Michael that night. There is no doubt in my mind that if Michael knew one person in the car would have to die he would say, let it be me.

And there is no doubt in my mind these words he wrote to Sam reflect the message he would want to share with you guys if he were standing here tonight.

You guys were a special part of Michael's life here on earth, and you will always be a special part of mine.

You guys will be part of many teams as you move forward in life.

The lesson Michael would want all of you to learn is any team is better with more love and more Jesus.

I love you guys."

Every player and parent in the room stood and applauded.

CHAPTER 41

● ● ● ● ● ● ●

A Saturday Morning with Michael

I slowly drove Michael's black Toyota Tundra down the paved path running through the middle of the Gridley cemetery.

I reached into the passenger seat, grabbing my Bible and the plastic bag containing four brand new official Wilson game baseballs and a black Sharpie marker. I glanced at the Titleist backpack, still filled with books and sitting in the corner where he left it his last day at school.

I walked the now familiar path from the truck toward the road serving as the east boundary of the peaceful country cemetery. I paused at the pine tree just a few feet away from Michael's grave, admiring the rays of morning sun peeking through the branches and the cloudless bright blue sky.

I dropped to one knee when I reached his headstone, admiring the beautifully designed and crafted tribute.

Tears swelled as they always do when I look at the photos so beautifully etched and blasted into the exquisite black granite.

Michael in a baseball cap, flashing that precious smile for the camera with our Jeezy's pit bull paw lovingly draped over Michael's arm as they both mugged for the camera; Michael in the Heartland baseball uniform he was so proud of wearing; in his Normal West uniform making a diving catch; Michael on the golf course, holding a pose as he stared down a wedge into the green; a family photo with Kelly, Jimmy, Michael and me at our last Easter family dinner together.

Michael's quote from his own obituary he wrote in 2009 as part of our "Dare to be Uncommon" book study together; "I was a strong believer in Jesus Christ and helped others look to follow God."

Philippians 4:13, his favorite bible verse, etched in dark black against the gray background.

Loving son to Jim and Kelly; trusted brother to Jimmy; beloved Grandson; loyal friend to many.

And of course, Michael Collins: May 20, 1991 – April 2, 2014.

I took one baseball from the bag and wrote "2014 U Pioneers, 25-13."

I carefully placed it on the black granite base and took another ball out. I wrote "Regional Champions 2014."

I placed it next to the first ball and removed the third ball from the bag. I wrote "Sweet Sixteen 2014" and carefully placed it next to the first two.

I removed the final ball from the bag and wrote, "We Believe." I kissed the ball and gently placed it next to the other three.

I bowed my head, closed my eyes, and prayed aloud.

"Father God, thank you for the 22 years I had with Michael on this earth. He was such a blessing in our lives. Thank you for giving me the strength to go back and coach this season. I pray I was able to glorify you. I pray the young men on this team continue to grow closer to you. Please continue to watch over those kids. I pray this all in Jesus name. Amen."

Still on one knee, I opened my bible. I turned to where I was last in my intended daily reading from the gospels, Matthew 28:16. I began to read aloud.

> "Then the eleven disciples left for Galilee, going to the mountain where Jesus had told them to go. When they saw Him, they worshiped Him – but some of them doubted!
> Jesus came and told his disciples, "I have been given all authority in heaven and on earth. Therefore, go and make disciples of all the nations, baptizing them in the name of the Father and the Son and the Holy Spirit. Teach these new disciples to obey all the commands I have given you. And be sure of this: I am with you always, even to the end of the age."

I looked up at the headstone, drawn to the number 19 on Michael's Heartland Hawk jersey.

Since Michael's passing, we constantly look for signs somehow telling us he is ok and watching over us. Often those signs seem to have his beloved "19" attached to them.

I had just received another one.

I looked back at my bible. I re-read the 19th verse of Matthew 28 aloud again.

> "Therefore, go and make disciples of all nations, baptizing them in the name of the Father and the Son and the Holy Spirit."

I looked up and fixed my eyes once more on Michael's own words from his own obituary he had once penned.

"I was a strong believer in Jesus Christ and helped others look to follow God."

It felt like yet another piece of the puzzle.

"Michael," I said aloud, "I want to read you a letter I just received from Kendall Warner.

I pulled the hand-written letter from my back pocket, carefully unfolded it, and read aloud.

> *Coach Collins:*
>
> *Happy Fathers Day! I hope you have a great day!*
>
> *I am proud to say this year was the best year of baseball for me. Besides going 25-13, we made it to the Sectional Championship game! I just wanted you to know we would have never made it there without you. You weren't just a coach to us but also a father figure.*
>
> *All the rules you had when I joined varsity didn't make a lot of sense to me at first, it was just something I did. But now, after two years with you, I finally understand what they truly did for us as young men.*
>
> *The book you gave us really put things into perspective for me and many others as young men. Everything you talked about; practice as you play; doing things with a purpose; all correspond to main things we need in life. Everything you talked about and made us do, were things that helped us with baseball and life.*
>
> *I struggled at the beginning of the season, but if there is one thing I learned this season, I would say it's to never stop fighting and never give up.*
>
> *When you started talking about it's just the 36th game, when we were in the regional championship, it put things in perspective and helped us relax and just play baseball. Then when we made it to sectionals and you started talking about playing with house money — we had nothing to lose and I believe we played like it too! We all played our hearts out!*
>
> *There's a life lesson to be learned here and it's that things happen for a reason and God has a plan and we might not understand why He does some things but we just have to have a stronger faith. Sacred Heart might have won that game but I know we won truly because we are better now because of you.*
>
> *We faced a lot of adversity and I just want you to know I am proud of you for stepping back on the field and fathering us still.*
>
> *I know MC is extremely proud of you! I also feel like he is extremely proud of us too. I actually don't feel, I know he is.*
>
> *Thank you for everything you did, and for the best years of varsity baseball a kid could hope for. Have a Happy Fathers Day!*

Forever a Pioneer baseball player,
Kendall Warner

I closed my eyes and bowed my head. A warm and gentle breeze blew across the cemetery.

I felt Michael's arm drape across my shoulders.

"Those guys made me proud dad," he said. "What a great run."

I didn't speak, focused on the feel of his arm around me.

I so badly missed the warmth of my son's embrace.

"I'm proud of you for going back to coach Dad," he whispered. "I couldn't believe it when you said you wouldn't go back without me."

He had been unconscious when I whispered that to him in his hospital room.

"You loved them and led them like Jesus," he said. "Just like I said, more love, more Jesus."

He must have sensed the wheels in my head spinning to determine a response. He broke the silence with a question.

"Did you get any complaints from parents?" he asked, though his tone seemed to suggest he already knew the answer.

"Not a single one all season," I answered. "But not because they were always happy or agreed with me," I added. "They just knew how petty they would seem if they complained about playing time given what we were going through."

"They knew this team was learning something bigger than baseball," he stated matter-of-factly. "And hopefully, that is a lesson they will all carry with them."

"Did any players miss games because of code of conduct violations?" Michael continued.

"No," I replied.

"How about those core values?" he continued. "Did you feel like they were One Team?"

"Like no team I've ever seen before," I said.

"And mental toughness?" Michael asked.

"Are you kidding me?" I answered.

"They did love me," he said, smiling that ornery smile I missed so much.

"And you won a regional championship!" he exclaimed. "That was sweet! More than we expected when the season started!"

"It was quite a run," I beamed. "An incredible way to end the season. They deserved it."

"You did a great job with those kids dad," he beamed. "It was a perfect season."

"How could it be a perfect season Michael," I said. "You weren't here."

He chuckled.

"Dad, do you remember when you won the state championship game and I was on a bus headed back from the junior college world series?" Michael asked.

"Of course I remember it," I answered.

"I didn't miss it," he said. "I just wasn't there."

I was silent as I pondered a rebuttal.

"The Newsboys song and the shirts before the regional were a nice touch," he added, apparently sensing I needed some further proof of his presence.

I hesitated, wanting to ask more, but he interrupted me.

"I am always with you Dad, and you are always with me."

"We believe Dad, we believe."

EPILOGUE

· ● ● ● ● ● ● ·

At the end of July I received a call from the parent of a sophomore-to-be. His son had played on our freshmen summer team. He wanted me to know it was not a good experience. He said they lost most of their games and the competition wasn't very good.

He failed to mention his kid struggled to catch routine fly balls and hit a paltry .130 against that weak competition, but still got to play as much as everyone else because the focus on our summer team is development.

I resigned my position as head baseball coach the following week.

Still in a very fragile state, I was clearly not ready for the year-round grind of trying to run a baseball program the way I think it needs to be run, and the headaches that can come along with it.

It is a decision I have regretted many times since, because I know Michael wants me to be coaching.

I hope one day I am ready to return to the dugout.

In the meantime, I will pray.

I pray coaches, athletes, and parents will experience a perfect season; where coaches and players hug after a win, and after a loss; where parents and players worry more about what they can give to the team, rather than what they can get; where players and parents understand what they are learning is bigger than baseball; where parents hug their players after every game and every chance they get.

I would give anything for one more hug…

*** There Are No Words ***

The drunk driver who killed Michael received the maximum prison sentence allowed by law. She will serve at least the mandatory minimum 85% of her 14-year sentence.

The passenger in her vehicle is serving a three-year prison term for obstruction of justice.

Kelly and I are serving a life sentence.

When a woman's husband dies, she is called a widow. A surviving husband is called a widower.

Children who lose their parents are called orphans.

But what do you call a mom and dad who have to face the death of their child?

There is no description.

There are no words.

*** What If ***

As summer ended, Kelly met with Pastor Baker. We struggled in different ways but over similar issues; why Michael, our anger with God, and what does forgiveness look like in this tragedy.

We struggled to reconcile this tragedy with God's sovereignty.

Knowing I was going to meet with Pastor Baker as well, she didn't share all the details of their conversation, but she did share one exchange.

"My life verse has always been Romans 8:28," Kelly told him. "And we know that all things work together for good to those who love God, to those who are called according to His purpose."

"I don't think that can be my life verse any more," she added.

"Why not?" Mike challenged.

"Because I don't understand why this had to happen to Michael and how this can be good," she responded.

"What if one person comes to know Christ because of what happened to Michael," Mike asked.

"I don't think so," Kelly answered.

"How about one thousand?" he followed.

The questions had certainly made us both stop and think.

*** I Helped Others Look to Follow God ***

Just before Christmas, two of Michael's best friends, Jason and Brad, asked if they could stop by our house. They wanted to share a "Michael story" with us.

They spoke of a night just a few short months ago. The three of them were sitting in the basement room where Michael lived, enjoying a Saturday night together.

The rambling discussion of three carefree college students turned to a recent automobile accident and a high school student badly injured in the crash. Rumor had it the injured student could not walk or talk, and the prognosis for recovery was not good.

Through tears, Jason and Brad shared with us what Michael had said to them that night.

"If that's ever me, pull the plug. I know where I am going."

The comment had some impact on the two boys then. It had an even greater impact four months later as Michael lay in that hospital bed.

I think of Michael's impact on those young men. Their walk with Jesus is now stronger.

I think about my nephew Jon. Michael had shared with him he would often picture Jesus kneeling at the end of his bed and he would talk to Jesus about life, especially during difficult times.

I think of Michael's impact on Jon and his walk with the Lord.

I think of the players and coaches on our 2014 Pioneer baseball team and the impact Michael had on all of us.

*** Game Seven ***

The words "Game Seven" conjure up a variety of images for athletes and fans: the Celtics and Lakers in several iconic NBA Finals match-ups for basketball supremacy; Sandy Koufax shutting out the Twins on two days rest and with torn ligaments in his elbow to win the 1965 World Series; Bill Mazeroski and his epic home run to beat the Yankees in the 1960 World Series, still the only Game Seven walk-off HR in World Series history.

Many different phrases also come to mind when athletes and fans hear the words "Game Seven" uttered: win or go home; one and done; do or die.

I now have a much different image haunt me when I think of "Game Seven."

My precious 22-year-old Michael, surrounded by his family, taking his final breath here on this earth.

I think back to his own obituary he wrote in his own words. I recall him horribly sick with the flu and asking if we would read the Bible to him. I think of him talking to Jesus at the foot of his bed.

He was ready for his true Game Seven moment.

I pray that you are too.

His story is not finished.

ACKNOWLEDGEMENTS

Chapter 1

Kindred, Randy. "Baseball puts Collinses on emotional ride." The Daily Pantagraph (Bloomington, IL), 3 June 2012. Reprinted with permission.

Chapter 33

Dungy, Tony. "The One Year Uncommon Life Daily Challenge." Tyndale House Publishers, Inc., 2011

Chapter 35

Kindred, Randy. "Michael Collins still guiding U High players." The Daily Pantagraph (Bloomington, IL) 13, April 2014. Reprinted/Adapted with permission.